Diocese of Peterborough
Youth Work and
Training Resources
Tel : 01604 887000

IN SIX DAYS

A.E. Turner

MINERVA PRESS

LONDON

MONTREUX   LOS ANGELES   SYDNEY

ISBN 1 86106 235 4

First Published 1997 by
MINERVA PRESS
315–317 Regent Street
London W1R 7YB

2nd Impression 1999

Printed in Great Britain for Minerva Press

IN SIX DAYS

For in six days the Lord made heaven and earth, the sea, and all that in them is, and rested the seventh day: wherefore the Lord blessed the sabbath day, and hallowed it.

Exodus 20:11

Contents

Chapter One
In The Beginning God

In the beginning God created the heaven and the earth.

Genesis 1:1

These are arguably the most famous ten words in all literature. No attempt is made to amplify them or to explain them. Sublimely simple and simply sublime they state a basic fact. When we read them we either accept them or we reject them. If we think that there is no such person as God then plainly this statement is at best misleading and at worst a deliberate lie. If we think that God does not exist then we will reject the statement as untrue. How can God create anything if he does not exist? Clearly then we will go no further in trying to understand it because it is just not true. In the Bible to believe something we first accept the statement as true and then proceed to try to understand it. Some people think that they have to understand it first and then be able to say that they believe it. The opposite is the case. Accept a statement as being true and reliable and then try to fathom what it fully means.

On the study of Logic we approach a matter with a few basic questions, such as *when, who, what, why* and *where*. The first sentence of the Bible tells us:

(1) When – in the beginning
(2) Who – God
(3) What did He do – He created
(4) What did He create – Heaven and the Earth.

The *why* does not arise because we have no idea why He did it except for his own pleasure. God just loves creating new things. The *where* does not apply either because it covers the whole of the universe.

Accepting this as a true statement we pass on to ask further questions. The first is *what* does it mean by "the beginning"? Is it the beginning of time? No. Time is relative to the sun and the constellations. Time could not begin to be counted until there was a solar system and constellations for it to pass through. Days, months and years could not begin until there was a sun around which the Earth could revolve. Nights could not begin until there was a moon with phases around which months could be calculated. We have to go back then to a period before time as we know it began.

The beginning of Creation then? No. Everything material must have a beginning. Every mountain, every ocean, every star had to begin somewhere. If a thing was made then something or someone had to make it so we need to go back even earlier than the making of the first star. In point of fact we need to go right back to a time when there was nothing but empty Space. And that is exactly where the Bible story begins, with this vast universe just an empty Space. One cannot go back any further than that. In the beginning is therefore the very beginning of all things.

We then come to the next question. Who then is God? The atheist will then say that as God does not exist the universe must just have happened accidentally and made itself with neither purpose nor design. Other people think about it and come to the conclusion that God is an abstract name for the laws of Nature. Take two parts of hydrogen and one of oxygen and you have water. That is a law of Nature. On the other hand take four parts of nitrogen and one of oxygen and you have breathable air, capable of sustaining life. So we have another law of Nature which does not need the hand of God to come about. The law of gravity compels one object to be pulled towards another automatically. These kind of laws work together and once again there is no need to have a Supreme Being in control planning and causing things to happen. Natural laws cause things to happen by themselves. This notion is an extension of atheism and merely substitutes Nature for God. The text would then read: 'In the beginning Mother Nature created the Heaven and the Earth.'

Let us then assume that the reader is prepared to accept that this is a plausible interpretation of the opening verse and therefore with an abstract thing being seen as God we can accept the statement as being reliable and true. We can now read on.

Now the name God appears forty-seven times in the first chapter of Genesis. We are not going to list them all but most readers are familiar with the chapter to a lesser or greater degree. A number of phrases keep on cropping up. For instance, there is the most frequent, "and God said". It would be very difficult to miss this because it comes in nearly every verse. As we read through the chapter this phrase will stick in our minds. God said, God said, God said. Surely this means that God has a voice and can speak? Now I know that you can look at a clock, whether ordinal or digital, and it will tell you the time without uttering a word. Now it is you that does the reading and understanding. I know also that many blind people have a talking clock or watch in which if you press a button a voice will actually tell you what the time is, but this is because there is a computer inside which is so programmed. God puts words into intelligible sentences and phrases. Clearly then there is a mind behind the voice which makes up coherent speech. Personally I do not know of any blend of hydrogen, nitrogen, oxygen or any other gas which can make up a sentence or phrase or command. God must have a mind and some sort of mouth.

Furthermore we read, "and God saw" at least seven times. God is therefore capable of seeing, observing and comprehending fully what He has seen. Once again we are forcibly shown that God has a mind and eyes of some sort that can take notice of things happening around. The law of gravity does not see anything, it simply exerts a force which is stronger than other forces and so pulls things down towards the Earth. It does not see the tree lose the apple and immediately pulls it towards the ground. The force just works automatically.

Notice again the phrase "and God said, Let".

"And God said, Let there be light."

"And God said, Let there be a firmament."

"And God said, Let the waters under heaven be gathered together into one place and let the dry land appear."

"And God said, Let the earth bring forth grass."

And so it goes on right down the chapter. Each time God spoke it was to give permission for something to happen. God has a mind, therefore, that is capable of making decisions to allow things to take place and of making sure that they happen.

We go on to read "and God divided". God then has a mind and will strong enough not only to make things happen but to separate one force from another. He divided the light from the darkness and called the light day and the darkness night.

God divided the waters which were under the firmament from the waters which were above the firmament. We shall see what this means later on but for the moment it is sufficient to notice that God not only spoke and allowed things to happen but that he had a mind that was always in total control of what was taking place. Let us look again; "and God made". He made trees and herbs, He made the sun and moon and the stars. He made man in his own image. Let us leave the understanding of what He did and how He did it until later on. Just accept for the moment that as though He had a pair of hands he actually took some material and manufactured these things. Finally, "God created". To make a thing you have to have some materials to use. To create is to bring something into being out of nothing and to start something absolutely new. So God created the Heavens and the Earth. He created great sea creatures. He created birds to fly in the air. He created many kinds of animals to walk and creep on the land and finally He created man in his own image. If He starts with no materials and creates something then God has first to make the materials which He intends to use.

Quite clearly then God has a mind, He can speak with a voice, He can see and understand fully. He can make decisions and see that they are carried out to His entire satisfaction. He can manufacture things on a massive scale and He can create new things which were never there previously. The forces of Nature cannot do any of these things of themselves. God must be some kind of living being with a mind of immense proportions far beyond the range of mortal man. What kind of being can this possibly be? It seems therefore that the theory that God is an abstract thing and merely a general name for natural forces is not a tenable theory. It is blown out of the window by the end of the first chapter in the Bible. God is not a thing but a being and one with a vastly superior intelligence such as we on Earth have never encountered. Having failed to come up with a satisfactory answer we are still left with the question: Who then is God?

*

As good Bible students we look in the Hebrew Dictionary to find the word used for God. It is *Elohim*. Now *Elohim* is the plural of *El* the Almighty One or the All Powerful One and is frequently used for God in the Old Testament but printed in all capital letters. Since *Elohim* is plural it really means The Almighty Ones, and the first verse could literally be translated, "In the beginning the Almighty Ones created the heaven and the earth." However before we jump to the wrong conclusion we see that later on in the chapter we read:

"And God said, Let *us* make man in *our* image". You notice that He does not say, "I will make man in *my* image". There is therefore consultation between two or more Beings. But He goes on to add that He made man in His own image.

Who then, you may well ask, does the one great invisible spirit which we call God consult with?

To answer this, we have to turn to the witness of John the Apostle who was a cousin of Jesus, their two mothers being sisters. John would grow up with Jesus as a boy and would know a lot about him. We are not entering into controversy about who wrote the Fourth Gospel. Traditionally it is ascribed to John and there is no point in arguing it two thousand years later.

John does not tell of the birth in Bethlehem and the visit of the shepherds. Nor does he tell of the Wise Men and their visit to Nazareth some months later. John goes right back to the same beginning as Genesis.

In the beginning was the Word, and the Word was with God, and the Word was God.
The same was in the beginning with God.

John 1:1

Once more we adopt the principle that what John wrote was true and that he certainly believed that what he was writing was true as dictated by the Holy Spirit. Nothing in the Bible is invented by the writer. Nothing is fiction.

In the beginning then we have empty Space and God, whoever He turns out to be. With him in full equality and full partnership was a person called the Word. He is the expression of all the thoughts in the mind of God and all the purposes in His heart.

The Word was equal with God and was God in His own right, having all the qualities skill and power and wisdom of God. He was in the beginning of Creation in partnership with God. This person, says John, is the Word who was made flesh. He was in the world and the world was made by Him and the world knew Him not. This is a most remarkable statement and if we accept it as true, which we must do, then in that beginning He was there and He actually did the creating. Whatever happened He is the one who knew.

Over thirty years later when Jesus talked with the woman (John 4:24) he said God is a spirit.

One must admit that we humans know very little about the world of spirits. We call it the paranormal and readily agree that there are more things in Heaven and Earth than we know about. We know a little of poltergeists. They are spirits that occasionally get a bit rowdy and pick things up and throw them across the room. It is no use denying that they exist and it is equally useless pretending that we understand what goes on. They are spirits and seem to have minds of their own. Spirits are normally associated with the departed and once again in all the stories we read about there seems to be a little truth and a lot of fiction. What do we know from the Bible about the world of spirits?

1. A spirit is *indestructible*. No one not even God can kill a spirit. It cannot be knifed, bombed, strangled, poisoned nor can a sprit be clubbed or beaten to death. In fact a spirit once it comes into being is immortal. Hebrews 12:9 asks us to be in subjection to the Father of spirits even more than to our fathers according to the flesh. So here is a thought then that God is the Father of all spirits, both good and bad. They have all come from one great original source which once started is indestructible. Yes, part of each one of us humans is indestructible. Jesus once said that God can destroy both the soul and the body in Hades, but not the spirit (Matthew 10:28).

2. A spirit is *invisible*. Occasionally, a spirit of someone departed is said to materialise but in the normal course of things the spirit is invisible both during the lifetime and after the death of the body. You never actually see the spirit. No man has seen God at any time says John in the first chapter of his Gospel. The only begotten Son who dwells in the embrace of the Father has declared Him. But if a spirit is invisible it does fill all the space that it is in. While filling all the universe this great invisible Spirit is known to be *omnipresent*. That simply means that God is everywhere and sees everything. Can you conceive of a spirit big enough to fill all the Heavens and Earth and so be present everywhere all the time? God then is not a person with a head, torso, arms and legs. He is a great invisible Spirit that is *omnipresent* – which means he is everywhere.

*Whither shall I go from your spirit? Or whither shall I
flee from your presence?*
*If I ascend up into heaven you are there: if I make my
bed in hell, behold you are there.*
*If I take the wings of the morning, and dwell in the
uttermost parts of the sea;*
Even there shall your hand lead me
And your right hand shall hold me.

Psalm 139:7-10

3.   God is also *infallible*. That is to say he is the source of all
knowledge and all wisdom. Let us quote to you Isaiah 40:13.

*Who has directed the spirit of the Lord, or being his
counsellor has taught him?*
*With whom took he counsel, and who instructed him,
and taught him the path of judgement, and taught him
knowledge, and showed to him the way of
understanding?*

The Lord had no one to consult and no one to advise Him. There
were no reference books for Him to use. He had to know the right
way to do things. He had to have all scientific knowledge and know
all the laws of Nature. He had to understand what would happen if
He blended certain gasses together, and what would not happen.

The upshot of all this is the realisation that all knowledge and
wisdom begins with God. You cannot go any further back because He
had no one to consult and there is no higher authority to advise or
control him. All knowledge therefore begins in the great invisible
Spirit which we call God.

He is said to be *omniscient*.

Everything past, present and future is within the circumference of
His knowledge and wisdom. This is the great invisible Spirit that we
call God, ever-present and all-seeing as well as all-knowing.

But there came a moment in time when the first change occurred.
The invisible Spirit which filled all Space and could see and know
everything became visible. With the emergence of a God who could
be seen if there had been anyone there to see Him, we have a new
phrase introduced in Scripture.

God is light.

Let us quote a few words from Psalm 104 which is the other main account of the Creation.

Bless the Lord O my soul; O Lord my God you are very great; you are clothed with honour and majesty.
Who coverest yourself with light as with a garment; who stretchest out the heavens like a curtain.

Psalm 104:1-2

God has made a move to be seen by clothing Himself with honour and majesty. He is said to have covered Himself with light as with a garment and then proceeded to stretch out the Heavens like the curtains of a tent for Him to live in. The idea of the Heavens being a tent for Him to dwell in is repeated by Isaiah 40:22, but we are not going to pursue that line of thought at the moment. Our minds are taken up with the statement that He covered Himself first with honour and majesty and then with a light as a cloak.

The Apostle Paul writing to Timothy in 1 Timothy 6:16 presents this thought concerning the Lord Jesus Christ who is King of Kings and Lord of Lords.

Who only has immortality, dwelling in light which no man can approach unto; whom no man has seen nor can see: to whom be honour and power everlasting. Amen.

The invisible God dwells in light to which no man can approach and is covered with honour and power or authority. These are remarkable words. The Lord Jesus Christ after His triumphant emergence from the tomb has returned to the invisible God from whence He came. That God in the beginning first clothed Himself with honour or glory and majesty or power and with light. In that same light the saints will dwell according to Colossians 1:12, but we are not going to go into that here.

The notion that God first was seen as a bright shining light comes in Hebrews 1:3.

The first visible appearance of God was as a bright and shining light who was the express image of His Person. This means literally translated that the light was the exact reproduction of the character and personality of the invisible God. The visible God thinks, speaks and acts exactly like the original invisible God. God calls Him His Son in Hebrews 1:2, John calls him the Word in the first chapter of his Gospel. The full and precise expression of the innermost thoughts of

God. Solomon calls him Wisdom in Proverbs 8, "and He did embody all the Wisdom of His Father the Invisible God." (Proverbs 8:12-31)

Speaking of the man they nailed to Calvary's cross, Paul says:

Who is the image (eikon) of the invisible God: the firstborn of all creation:
For by him were all things created, that are in the heaven, and that are in the earth.

Colossians 1:16

This is strong stuff you know. It challenges belief. But the fact is that when the light appeared and clothed the unseen God there emerged glory and power beyond human capability. The visible God who was in fact the invisible God clothed with light went on to create the whole of this vast universe. How could He do this?

The unseen Spirit as we have noticed already, had the knowledge and skill to see and understand and make decisions. Now he has a garment of light. Light is heat and heat is energy. The light of God was so brilliant that it could give off rays and emissions to create all natural light such as daylight and starlight and any other form of created light. It could also become a furnace so hot that it could make atoms and split them and manufacture any gasses or molecular structures needed to create planets, solar systems, galaxies and constellations. In other words God as the invisible Spirit and the visible Son has all the power, resources, knowledge and ability inside Himself to make anything He chooses. God does not have to go outside of Himself for anything with regard to Creation. He possesses all the resources once He had clothed Himself with the light.

Light produces heat which in turn produces electrical energy and nuclear energy. There are other forms of energy one of which is the wind. God has that as well. The Hebrew word for Spirit is *ruach* which means breath or wind. When we add the Spirit to the Father and the Son we have a totally irresistible Trinity of power and wisdom. God can breathe out with the force of a gentle breeze or of the greatest hurricane the universe has ever seen.

This breath is the breath of life breathed into Adam which leads us to the most amazing statement made about God. John, as we have seen, describes in his first chapter the Word who was with God and was God. This Word created all things by Him and for Him and nothing was made without Him. John then goes on to say "in him was life". Think about it. All life in the universe comes from a single source, namely the Word, which we call God. Every tree, every bird, every fish, every creature, was made alive. Man can take the egg from a woman and the sperm from a man and put them together in a dish in the laboratory and those two tiny speckles will mate. But they both have to be *alive*. Man cannot manufacture one single egg or he would be able to make a society all of his own choosing. He cannot make a daffodil bulb in a factory and plant it and see it grow. Down to the tiniest blade of grass or microbe, you have to begin with something that is alive. The original source of life is God Himself. You could make a rocky asteroid out of molten lava but there would be nothing alive on it without God. Men have argued for centuries about which came first – the chicken or the egg? They should have looked into Genesis 2! It tells them that the chicken was first. What does it matter? Whichever came first had to be alive; a chicken that can lay eggs containing the embryo of another chicken; a tree bearing fruit with the seeds of several more trees inside it – God is the origin and giver of life.

Let me quote some words of Paul in an address to thinking men on Mar's Hill in Athens long ago and recorded in Acts 17:24.

> *God that made the world and all things therein, seeing that he is Lord of Heaven and Earth, dwelleth not in temples made with hands;*
> *neither is worshipped with men's hands as though he needed any thing, seeing he giveth to all life, and breath, and all things;*

This is the appeal of Paul to the university professors and graduates of his day and to all thinking men of all ages. God is light. Without Him we would be living in total darkness because He once said: Let there be light.

In God is life, without God there would be no life of any sort. God has knowledge and has given us brains to acquire some of the knowledge which He possesses.

And God is love. We are not going to dwell on this here but just think that love is part of the nature of God and He has made man with the ability to love. This comes up for consideration when we look at what is meant by God making man in His own image. And so God is *omnipresent* because He as a spirit is able to be everywhere.

God is *omniscient* because He has all knowledge of all facts – past, present and future.

God is *omnipotent* because with His clothing of light He has the energy and facilities to produce any gas or material needed to create as many solar systems as He likes.

This is the picture given to us of God the Creator. Not a human being with limitations but a great Spirit with a presence and a mind, clothed in light which gives Him power and from whom emanates a Spirit or breath of life. The universe began with a ball of light and fire under the control of a superior mind. God is a living being.

Our trouble is that knowing that man is the greatest creature on this planet, we forget that Earth is one tiny part of the universe and that there has to be a being that is far greater in knowledge, wisdom and power than mortal man. That being we call God:

> *Now unto the Kin, eternal, immortal, invisible, the only*
> *wise god be honour and glory for ever and ever Amen.*
>
> 1 Timothy 1:17

A little poem will itemise some of the things that come from God. Obviously if there is no God then there is no Son of God and he can never be our Father because He does not exist. If we accept that God is light then we must see that without God there is no light.

Who Needs God Anyway?

No God, no love. It's as simple as that
It is sad but it is true.
If you live in God, you live in love
And God will live in you.
Human love takes many forms
There is no end to the list
For God is love and love is of God
Without God love would not exist.

No God, no light. What an awful thought!
The prospect should appal.
For God is light, His Word declares
And in Him is no darkness at all.
His opening words ring loud and true
And God said, Let there be light.
His closing words are equally great,
And there shall be no more night.

No God, no life and that is a fact
It knocks all theories flat.
In Him was life says John, Chapter One
And few can argue with that.
Everything created from grass to man
Had to have life to start
God is the only source of life.
He alone has life to impart.

No God, no Son, no Salvation
No Creator to worship or bless.
No Faith no Hope, no Eternal Life
No Father to turn to in stress.
Eternal Life is the highest form
Which all who possess it cherish.
Jesus gives it to all of His sheep
And none will ever perish.

Chapter Two
The World That Then Was

For... By the word of God the heavens were of old, and the earth standing out of the water and in the water:
Whereby the world that then was, being overflowed with water, perished.

2 Peter 3:5-6

At the age of seven, in June 1931, my father explained to me that God so loved me that He gave His only begotten Son to die for me, and that if I believed in Him I would have everlasting life. I believed what he had read to me from the Bible and so accepted the Lord Jesus Christ as my own personal Saviour. That is a lovely phrase which unfortunately has gone almost out of fashion. All the same, whether you call it being saved or being born again, I received Christ into my life.

The elders at the Gospel Hall where I was brought up taught me that God created the whole of this vast universe in six days and that He did it approximately six thousand years ago. Well, at that age if someone reads you a verse from the Bible and tells you that this is what it means you believe them. After all, they had believed what was told to them forty or fifty years previously and had been so busy preaching the Gospel that they had never questioned whether this was true or not.

When I was thirteen I was baptised by immersion and received into the fellowship, a year later I began to preach the Gospel myself. By that time I was fourteen and ready to leave school. Part of the matriculation exemption curriculum was Religious Knowledge. The science master doubled up as R.K. Teacher. He was an atheist. The book to study was First Samuel. I well remember that in one of the very first lessons he said that some people thought the Bible was somehow divinely inspired. He could not hold that belief since he simply looked upon the Bible as a collection of myths, legends fables and folklore written by men three or four thousand years ago who were superstitious and did not know any better. Obviously, we live in a much more enlightened age now and are much better informed! I was thirteen and recall very vividly a discussion with him in front of the class in which I defended the Scriptures and put forward my firmly held view that every word was written by holy men who were moved by the Holy Spirit. It was a good witness for Jesus Christ but I do not think I convinced him.

By the time I left school I was already hearing that science had absolutely undeniable and irrefutable evidence that the Earth was millions of years old and that there had been some form of life on it a very long time before Adam appeared on the scene. By the time I was called up into the Army at eighteen I had learned a lot about the opposing point of view and had many debates. There was ample evidence that the present human race appeared nearly six thousand years ago. The Jews work it out as 5,755 years in September 1994. There is no evidence of any civilisation, roads or colonisation prior to that date.

So I became aware that there was a war of words going on between the scientist and the theologian. If the latter sticks to the belief that the whole universe began when Adam was created then there is clear conflict between the two. Either the Bible was not telling the truth or the godly men who taught me had not understood what the Bible was actually saying.

In the harder school of an Army barracks I learned one of the greatest lessons of my life: there is a big difference between scientific facts and the theories built on them. And there is an equally big gap between Bible facts and the theories about them. Scientific facts and Bible facts will always be in agreement, I concluded, even at that age. Scientific theories and Bible theories may differ widely. The Bible cannot be wrong if holy men did indeed write as they were moved by the Holy Spirit. Bible statements are facts. Bible theories are the opinions of men trying to understand those facts. I have since found that some little things that those godly men told me were in fact just not true at all. But one thing they always stressed upon me. Never take for granted what you are told the Bible means. Read it for yourself. And so I accept that whatever is written or spoken about the Bible represents the opinions of the writer or speaker. Check it out and believe what you yourself read in the Scriptures. It is on this basis that this little book is written so that what the Bible actually says about the Creation may be considered. Personally, I consider that the scientist when taking the facts unearthed by digging and by the microscope or telescope should also take on board what is written in the Scriptures. He will save himself an awful lot of trouble if he just listens to what the Bible says. Similarly, the theologian ought to take on board the significance of scientific facts for they cannot be denied. Dinomania is now at its peak. Much of it is commercial hype designed to get people to go to the cinema. But at Jurassic Park scientists are studying hard to unravel the secrets of that bygone age when dinosaurs ruled the world and the ages before that when the ice melted. I want to show you that these facts are not in the least inconsistent with the teaching of the Word of God.

The Bible was written over a period of some sixteen hundred years or so, by forty or more men who had only one thing in common. They all believed that God had something to say through them and so they put pen to parchment and wrote at the dictation of the Spirit of God. Most of them had no claim to scholarship or theological ability. Take for instance Simon Peter. He was a rough, rugged fisherman of Galilee who could not read or write. A relative of his named John Mark wrote his Gospel for him and his First Letter was dictated to Silvanus, also known as Silas the friend of Paul.

When towards the end of his life Peter wrote his Second Letter he tells of truth made known to him regarding the universe in the third chapter. It is dramatic and sensational and I do not believe that Peter was mentally capable of making it up for it puts modern science fiction in the shade.

God had revealed future truth to Paul concerning the Church which is the Body of which Christ is the Head. This takes the Church into the ages to come. To Peter was revealed the basic truth regarding the universe, from the beginning right into those same eternal ages. From Peter we learn that the history of the world is in three stages.

1. *The Heavens which were of old* including the Earth which then stood out of the water and in the water; in other words the Earth was one continent and one ocean.

Peter then tells of a cataclysmic disaster which overtook the Earth and destroyed all life on the planet by a flood. This ties up with the second verse of Genesis 1:2, where we first find the Earth as all in darkness and all under water.

2. *The Heavens and the Earth which are now.*

Peter then details the present arrangement of the Heaven and the Earth as temporary measures. Day and Night, Sun and Moon and Summer and Winter are all for the time being only. They were not there before and will not be there when the present period has ended.

The Heavens and the Earth are described as being held in store pending the Day of Judgement by fire. Peter graphically describes the Heavens being on fire and the elements melting with intense heat.

3. *The new Heavens and the new Earth.*

Having made satisfactory arrangements for the people who have lived on Earth to be re-housed God will introduce an entirely new Earth and a new Heaven. The people who are saved will live on that new Earth for ever. The people who are lost will be... well lost. If you read the last two chapters of Isaiah and the last two chapters of Revelation you will learn more about the New Heavens and New Earth. It is not part of our purpose in this book to enlarge on that period except to say that it will last for ever, without whatever it was caused the disaster, as we will call it from now on.

So there was a long period of time between the first two verses of the Bible. The story of the original Creation occupies just one verse. In the beginning God created the Heavens and the Earth. That is about all the Bible is going to say on the subject. God will not tell you how He did it, nor how long ago it was nor how long it took Him. That is open to the scientist to discover. Whatever science unearths about the pre-historic period the Bible will not argue because it is silent on the matter. God actually wants man to find out all he can, which is why God has given him such an enquiring mind.

While we have no details of the various forms of life on this planet previously to man we do have some very important clues!

Clue Number One

And, thou, Lord in the beginning hast laid the foundation of the earth.
Hebrews 1:10

The clue here is in the words 'In the beginning'. It is exactly the same beginning as in Genesis 1:1. From its mention here we conclude that the Earth has existed in some form or other right from the very start of the Creation programme. It is easy to imagine that after creating a few million stars God eventually got round to making a further solar system containing the planet Earth. Nothing could be further from the truth! The Earth seems to have begun its journey as one of the first batch of stars to be born and as an independent planet and not part of a solar system. We will come back to this later when we consider that the sun and moon did not appear in the skies above the Earth until the fourth day.

Clue Number Two

The foundation of the earth.

Hebrews 1:10

This verse is a quotation from Psalm 102:25 and is very significant. Does not the word 'foundation' suggest that the Earth has been built in stages? The picture in my mind of digging out the footings in order to lay a foundation on which the intended house can be erected is a very good picture. The Earth appears not to have been in the same size and shape as it is now when it was first made. If it did come off a nebula and then cooled down we have a hard core as a foundation from which the Earth itself has evolved or developed. Perhaps because of the frequent emissions of molten lava through volcanoes the centre of the Earth has not totally cooled even yet? Maybe a hard core formed around the molten hot centre?

The notion of a foundation for the Earth is very common in Scripture. Let me remind you of three things that are said to belong to the period prior to its foundation.

Jesus said in prayer to His Father: *thou lovest me before the foundation of the world.* The world is the cosmos as created and the Father and Son existed prior to the first star being made. They loved each other which is where love started in the universe. It is great to think that love is older than the world itself.

Peter in his First Letter and the first chapter speaks of *the Lamb ordained to be slain before the foundation of the world.* Thus we learn that Calvary was planned before the Earth began to be made.

Paul in the Letter to the Ephesians (1:4) writes of the Church the Body of Christ being chosen *before the foundation of the world.*

So we see that before the first rock was formed in the making of planet Earth God had and loved a Son. His death on Calvary as a sacrificial Lamb for the world was determined and the intention of having a Church with God throughout all eternity to come was also made into a firm Purpose of God.

Clue Number Three

The Heavens were of old, and the earth...

2 Peter 3:5

Of old Lord hast thou laid the foundation of the earth.

Psalm 102:25

The two words 'of old' provide the third clue. They are common in both Old and New Testaments although not always obvious in the English translation. Let me explain. In the New Testament the two words 'eternal' and 'everlasting' are interchangeable. They are the rendering of the same Greek word which is *aion*. This simply means an age of any length.

In the Old Testament, however, they are two different words.

Moses in Deuteronomy 33:27 concludes his blessing of the nation of Israel with these words:

> *The Eternal God is thy refuge and underneath are the everlasting arms.*

The first word 'Eternal' means the God of the ages that are now ceased, while the word 'Everlasting' means the ages that are yet to come of which no end is in view.

We find these same two words together again in Psalm 90:2, "from everlasting to everlasting thou art God." From the ages that are now past and ceased to the ages that are yet to come Thou art God. This is the theology of the man Moses and who can disagree with him? From these and many other occurrences of the same two words we learn that God is indeed the God of ages past. Assuredly, this entitles us to form the opinion that the Earth has not only developed in stages but has passed through a number of ages in the purposes of God. Yes what science discovered the Bible had been saying all along. There have been ages of evolution of the Earth. From the Ice Age through the Crustacean Age and on to the Dinosaur Age they are all allowed for in the Bible. The Earth itself has developed in stages and has evolved through many ages that have now ceased.

Clue Number Four

The earth was without, form and void; and darkness was upon the face of the deep.

Genesis 1:2

While the original Creation is in verse one, we have now come to the first picture of planet Earth. It is a dismal picture of desolation, darkness and deep waters. The clue is in the word 'was' because it is a tense of the verb 'to be'. It is properly translated 'the Earth became without form and void'. We shall see in the next chapter how it came to be waste and empty. For the moment we are thinking of what it was like previously. I would like to suggest some of the measures introduced in the remainder of the chapter form a picture of what the Earth had been like as it was created by God and passed through all its stages of evolution.

Firstly, it was not in total darkness. Previous to then it had been in continuous light. Peter warned (2 Peter 3) of the danger of assuming that all things continue as they were from the beginning. It is wrong to take for granted that because we now have day and night every twenty-four hours that there has always been alternating light and dark. In the Heavens and Earth of old there was unbroken daylight. Then there was a period of unbroken darkness. In the Heavens which are now they alternate. In the New Heavens and New Earth it will revert to continuous day. Light will have triumphed over the darkness and will then rule forever.

Secondly, the Earth is seen as void or empty; that is to say that there was no life on the planet. Death had taken over and everything from the smallest blade of grass to the largest dinosaur was dead. It had not always been so. God is a God of Life not Death. Therefore, it is not surprising that a hedgehog could grow to thirty feet in length. It could live for a thousand years. There was nothing to kill it. You see what we are driving at? Earth had no poisonous plants or insects. God had created nothing that could kill by being eaten. Animals did not prey upon smaller animals for food. Everything in the Earth was living, growing and prosperous. Life could only end when God himself withdrew the breath from a creature. Nothing was killed.

Hence dinosaurs started as small lizards and grew up to enormous length.

Life itself, if allowed to progress unhindered, is self-perpetuating. Once again what science discovered, the Bible already allowed for. During the pre-historic ages life simply went on producing new and higher forms of life. If a species was allowed to die out it was not before other forms of life had developed. God never says that from the beginning of Creation each form of life was created as a separate introduction. All that science says about evolution is almost certainly true during those ages. Even to the emergence of primates and possibly some primitive form of man.

Life on Earth for millions of years was positively blooming. No darkness, no death, and no disease or decay.

Thirdly, there was no sun or moon. Therefore, the Earth did not have the large variations in temperature that we know only too well. It was not freezing cold at the poles and blazing hot at the equator. Earth did not have summer and winter. It did not get cold and dark at the end of every day. Temperature throughout the planet would be constant and any change would be very slow. Perhaps one degree upwards every few thousand years as the Earth slowly emerged from the Ice Age. Scientists in the laboratory at Jurassic Park are working on the assumption that present variations in temperature have always operated. That is just not true.

If there was some primitive man, and there might have been, he was not in the image of God and we shall see later what exactly that phrase involves... he had no soul to save.

All this means that God had created the Earth as a separate independent planet and not part of a solar system. God himself being light provided all the light and heat that the Earth needed and allowed life to evolve under His own supervision.

And God was happy with what He saw. For millions of years life went on growing and blossoming with literally not a cloud in the sky. Perhaps working up to the point where man could be introduced to take charge. But as God in his wisdom and foreknowledge knew trouble was on the horizon. You see this was a world in which there was no evil, but things were to change.

Chapter Three
Enter the Villain

The only forms of life we know about for sure are here on Earth. Vegetation, aquatic life, bird life, animal life and human life. Apart from these there are of course microbes and bacteria and insects of one sort or another. Science has not found any evidence of life now on any other planet in our solar system and as for the rest of the Milky Way and the major constellations we cannot reach that far with our probes. But there is one other form of life in the universe that we definitely know about and that is Angelic Life. All that is known of these created beings is in our Bibles.

I know that a lot of people pour scorn on the idea of angels existing and link them with fairies and leprechauns. Nevertheless, the Bible is full of them from Genesis to Revelation and the people mentioned in the Scriptures always believed in them. They come on a level that is somewhere between Man and God in terms of capability and knowledge. So what does the Book tell us about angels?

Let me quote you a passage out of the Book of Job, probably the first book to be written.

> *The Lord answered Job out of the whirlwind...Where were you when I laid the foundations of the earth?...whereupon are the foundations fastened? or who laid the corner stone thereof; when the morning stars sang together and all the sons of God shouted for joy?*

Job 38:1-7

The morning stars is a name for a choir of angels. Who said musical groups were a modern thing? The sons of God are angels as also mentioned in Job 1 when they have to attend periodically in Heaven to give a report of what they have done.

It seems then that God made a number of angels and then started to make planets for them to live on. No wonder they shouted for joy and sang together!

Angels have to eat food. We know that because for forty years the Israelites were given angel's food made out of the hoar frost of the ground. It was white like coriander seed but could be ground to flour with the oil already mixed in it and it tasted like honey. Flour, fat and sweetness all in one seed. There is nothing like that grown on Earth.

We also know that angels are spirits like God himself. Their main function today is to minister to the spiritual needs of those who are heirs of salvation, namely the Christians. Yes, we believe in guardian angels according to Hebrews 1. Children have guardian angels and we know that from Jesus himself. "In heaven their angels do always behold the face of God." (Matthew 18:10)

Churches have angels since the seven letters of Revelation 2-3 are actually addressed to the angel of each church.

There is a hierarchy of angels and we know this from Colossians 1 where the Son of God created all things, visible and invisible, thrones and dominions, principalities and powers in Heaven and on Earth.

Just as there are levels of government on Earth and no leader can assume power unless God chooses to let him, so there are levels of government in the Heavens. Some angels have thrones, some have dominion over a whole group of stars, some are princes or chief rulers and some have power or authority. In Daniel 9 we learn that while Michael is the only Archangel named in the Bible there was also the Prince of Persia. Some angels seem to have responsibility for the affairs of a country or kingdom. From Job 1 we understand that discussions take place in Heaven and decisions are taken in heaven which result in actions taking place on Earth. Angels are involved in these discussions and decisions.

Angels throughout the Bible were messengers, and frequently came down to Earth to deliver messages from God. On some occasions these appearances were in dreams while on others the angel appeared literally. The angel usually assumed the appearance of a human being when he came to Earth and would be dressed like an ordinary man. Rarely, if ever, did the angel appear with outstretched wings and glowing with light. Since God has a vast universe to run He is able to send his messengers anywhere He chooses and there is no need for transport to be arranged. It appears that angels can disappear on one planet and appear instantly on another. Michael actually apologised to Daniel for taking three weeks to get to him with a message. The Prince of Persia had withstood him and did not want him to go.

Man has only been on the Earth for less than six thousand years while angels have been there from the beginning of Creation. God has a vast universe to run and the Earth is only one of millions of planets and one of the smallest. It may have been fifty million, five hundred million or five thousand million years ago when the angels rejoiced at the birth of the first batch of stars among which was planet Earth. The angels have been there all the time and there must be many other forms of life in other solar systems since God has a purpose in creating each individual star. Earth appears to have always been his favourite planet because on it were so many different forms of life all living and growing. Everything was peaceful and harmonious for millions of years and God was happy and delighted with all that was going on. Angels have one great limitation. They have superior minds to ours but do not have freedom of choice as we do. An angel does what he is told when he is told instantly. Gabriel has stood in the presence of God for the last six thousand years and has only done two things so far as the Earth is concerned. He came to tell Mary that she had been chosen to bring God's child into the world, and he came in a dream to tell Joseph that it was to be the Son of God. If an angel disobeys God he is finished. There is no way of repentance or forgiveness for him. In Genesis 6 angels came to Earth to do the business of God and saw the daughters of men. Having human bodies they were attracted to them and children were born, which were giants; they were neither divine nor human, but angelic. Those angels are reserved in chains in blackness until the day of their judgement (2 Peter 2:4).

Another difference between angels and men is that angels are each one created separately and do not have powers of procreation. God made each one separately and being spirits they cannot be killed. That is how God ran the universe since the beginning. They gathered regularly to worship God and they did His bidding instantly and served Him continually. God is called the Lord of Hosts frequently and the hosts are the hosts of angels. While the lower echelons of angels were servants, there was a group called seraphim. These were heralds and had trumpets to sound when some big event was to take place. One of them is waiting even now to sound the trumpet to call the saints and believers in Christ out of the graves. These have six wings. Two cover their faces because they are unable to gaze directly on the brilliant light of the glory of God. They have two wings to fly and two to cover their feet in humility. These are a special group of angels.

There is another small group which are even more select. They are called cherubim. A cherub is a special angel with wings, made by God for a special purpose. Two cherubim were placed on guard outside the Garden of Eden to make sure that no one in a state of sin entered the Garden and partook of the Tree of Life. Golden cherubim were woven into the curtains of the tabernacle and two solid gold cherubim sat or stood with their faces looking down on to the mercy seat to see that the blood of sacrifice was there so that no sinful priest might approach God in worship and the ordinary people might go about their business knowing that the sin offering of the atoning blood had been offered and accepted. Cherubim therefore guard the holiness of God and are made to keep sin and sinners out of the presence of God.

The leader of this select band of angels, which were in effect the royal guard, was called the anointed cherub. How do we know this? Can we again adopt the same principle as at the start of this book? Take a statement of Scripture and accept it on its face value as being a true and faithful statement and then begin to think what it means. This time we go to the prophet Ezekiel 28:14: "You are the anointed cherub that covers; and I have set you so." Anybody in Scripture who is anointed is specially chosen to do a specific job and appointed thereto like a priest or a king. This was one specially created to be the leader of the band of cherubim and God says that he had purposely placed him in that position. A cherub that covered was a cherub that guarded or protected. He was an angelic shield before God to keep away all trouble. The merest hint of an angel not willing to carry out the wishes of God and he would act firmly to snuff out any thoughts of rebellion. Who is this superior being? We are told several things about him. (All quotations from Ezekiel 28:12-20.)

You seal up the sum. This means that he was the tops, the last word, the greatest of the angels.

Full of wisdom. God had gifted him with all necessary wisdom to be able at all times to act wisely.

Perfect in beauty. God had made the most beautiful and attractive person He had ever created. Stunning good looks and commanding figure. Outstanding among the angels none of which would in themselves be ugly.

You have been in Eden the garden of God. As this describes something that took place millions of years before Genesis 3 the scholars are right to interpret this as referring to the whole Earth as one great Paradise garden in pre-historic days.

Every precious stone was your covering. Clothed in a garment of diamonds and every other precious stone including gold he would indeed be most beautiful.

The workmanship of your tabrets and of your pipes was prepared in you in the day you were created. His voice was like listening to a mighty cathedral organ and God had made it that way for him to lead the angelic choir when singing the praises and worship of God.

A mighty angel indeed, strikingly beautiful and melodious. But he also seems to have had privileges not available to other angels.

You have been in the holy mountain of God.
You have walked up and down in the midst of the stones of fire.

I honestly do not pretend to know what these phrases mean but I am sure that they refer to places in Heaven to walk in which was a great privilege indeed. Anything to do with holiness and fire with God is important. He who guarded the holiness of God was allowed to visit the mountain of holiness and to walk up and down between the burning stones.

You were perfect in all your ways till iniquity was found in you.

What a condemnation! So wise so beautiful so perfect as to be allowed to stand next to God himself and then iniquity was found in him.

What was the iniquity?

Your heart was lifted up because of your beauty.

Oh dear. Did he not with all his God given wisdom know that the one thing God cannot abide is pride?

By the multitude of your merchandise they have filled the midst of you with violence and you have sinned.

Curtains. He had been doing some trading and was so unwise as to think that God did not know. His pride led to violence, and in rebellion against God he had sinned.

Pride, attacking other angels, disobeying God. This could not be tolerated in the presence of a holy God and so he was cast out of Heaven and made to dwell in outer space.

I suggest you read this passage (Ezekiel 28:12-20) many times and you will find many answers.

Who is this person? To answer that question we have to turn back to Isaiah 14:12.

How are you fallen from heaven, O Lucifer, son of the morning!

If we compare this statement with that made by Jesus seven hundred years later we see a great truth.

I beheld Satan as lightning fall from heaven.

Luke 10:18

The name Satan means the adversary of God, while the name Lucifer means the day star. He who ought to have been the flagship star of God to herald the dawn of a new eternal day became instead the leader of all opposition to God and His will and ways.

His pride led to a fivefold ambition which proved his undoing.

For you have said in your heart:

1.   *I will ascend into Heaven.* (Isaiah 14:13-14)

It was rather like someone who has free access to Buckingham Palace and continually waits upon the Queen in service saying that he wanted to go and live in the Palace as a member of the Royal household. He can only do that if asked. Lucifer had no intention of going about things in a manner pleasing to God.

2.   *I will exalt my throne above the stars of God.*

He was not content to have a throne alongside several other angels. He wanted to be promoted above them all so that he could give them orders and take over the running of God's house. Ambition can be a terrible thing.

3. *I will sit upon the mount of the congregation in the Sides of the North.*

The mount of the congregation is a place reserved for the company of those who are saved from Earth by being declared righteous by God. We do not know where the sides of the north may be but perhaps it has something to do with the North Star in Ursa Major. Wherever it is, Psalm 1 speaks of the time when there will be a congregating together of the righteous. No sinner will be allowed to stand there. Saints will get there because they will have chosen to serve God and to please him in all their ways. Lucifer was not thinking of the way of love, joy and peace nor of gentleness, meekness and faith. Rather he was prepared to be selfish and to do whatever he wanted. Fighting, killing, robbing, lying and cheating were in his heart. Total rejection of the ways of the Lord. Yet, he still wanted to dwell in eternity to come with the saints in light. It just was not on.

4. *I will ascend above the heights of the clouds.*

To reach up and take a place in Heaven without accepting God as his Master could not be done but that is what he tried to do. Rejecting light, life and love he preferred darkness, death and hatred.

5. *I will be like the Most High.*

Perhaps this was the core of his ambition? Not content to be next to God and leading the worship of the angels he reached out for equality with the Almighty and for angels to worship him. What a contrast with the One who did not think it robbery to be equal with God but humbled himself and became obedient to death in Philippians 2.

What a crisis this must have been for God and his Son and Spirit! We do not know of course how much Lucifer knew of the purposes of God but he certainly knew that there was an area of the Heavens called the Sides of the North reserved for future occupation by a company known as The Righteous Ones. He may well have known of the plan ultimately to create a new type of creature in the image of God and to put him in charge of this planet. The Earth was the favourite garden planet of God and His delight has always been in it. Lucifer then might have been jealous and thought that maybe he should have the job. Since the man would be both male and female while angels are neither, Lucifer could have worked it out that mankind would breed rapidly on Earth and from their ranks would come those who would be righteous and take that meeting place in the Heavens. He might even have known of some sort of plan for a bride for the Eternal Son of God. Whatever the reason, things boiled up inside him and brought him to the point of revolt. Lucifer was not seeking to be like God in righteousness and love. He sought only position and the power it gave him over other angels. His methods of achieving and maintaining that position were far from the methods of God.

How are the mighty fallen we could well say. Here was an angel who wanted to be like God but had no wish to behave like God. No loving kindness for him. He wanted to join the ranks of the righteous in the ages to come but had no intention of trying actually to be righteous. Honesty did not always pay dividends. He aspired to the Sides of the North, but alas was cast down to the sides of the pit. Probably the most powerful angel of them all he is finally brought down to the grave where he is stripped of all powers. Kings of the Earth ask him, "Are you become weak like one of us?"

The crisis then was that from a created spirit had emerged for the first time an evil spirit. Evil is the opposite of good as hatred is the opposite of love. What was God to do? He could not destroy Lucifer because spirits are indestructible, as we have seen. He could lock him up or he could forbid to allow him to practise evil. But what is the use of telling a child not to be naughty again? I think parents can sympathise with God in his dilemma. God of course knew that it would happen and had already planned what to do about the situation. Thus he allowed Lucifer to assume the name of Satan the Adversary and to assert his evil influence on part of God's Creation.

This is what God decided to do. For a time good and evil must exist side by side with God himself monitoring the situation to see that evil was kept within strict bounds. The great battle had begun with God knowing the inevitable outcome.

On Earth life continued serene and calm. One land mass and one ocean. The latter had spawned a great variety of fishes but probably not as many forms as we know today since there was no man to catch and eat them. The land was covered in rich foliage. No trees such as we have today, that is to say no oak, pine or cedar trees and of the enormous range of pretty flowers which again need a man to cultivate. The daylight was continuous and the temperature even. With no sun or moon and no day or night temperatures nudged up slowly a degree every few thousand years as the Earth emerged from the Ice Age. The foliage was rich and succulent and the number of animals and birds multiplied. Over one hundred and fifty species of dinosaurs have been identified and they browsed as contentedly as a herd of cows munching the grass. All was peaceful, prosperous and progressive.

And then came a sinister change. Science has established that the early generations of dinosaurs were docile and friendly to one another. They fed on foliage and were truly gentle giants. But now a new breed of dinosaurs emerged that were aggressive, ferocious and hostile. They began to attack their fellow creatures and to vandalise the habitation. They attacked first for the sake of hurting and destroying, in order to show superiority over each other and then to kill for the sake of killing. Having killed, they started to eat the carcasses and eventually turned to killing for food alone. Science puts this down to a change between cold and warm blood, but as with so many other unpleasant things in the world the reason lies in the world of spirits. Satan was allowed to assert his evil influence over the animals and turn them into killers and destroyers. It is exactly the same evil spirit that has caused men in Bosnia who once lived in peace side by side, to turn on their neighbours and kill, rape and to seize and destroy their homes. The law of the jungle had entered and the source was the spirit turned evil, and preferring death to life, and strife to peace. Satan had embarked on the diametrically opposite course to the will and ways of the Lord. Original Sin had been committed in Heaven and was now poisoning the atmosphere of the Earth. I often used to wonder how sin could spoil the world when there was no man there to commit a sin? Now I understand that sin is the product of evil and that evil is everything that is harmful and bad. Evil is hatred and strife, lying and deceit. Evil is plants and insects that kill as well as humans. Cancer, blindness, mental disorders, and death are there in the world simply as a result of the presence and influence of Satan, the adversary of all the goodness of God.

God loves life: He is a conservationist and loves living and growing things. He detests death disease and decay. But He had to allow them up to a point. However, if He did not intervene in judgement, then the Pterodactyls, Triceratops and Tyrannosaurus Rex would eventually destroy all life on this planet and all trace of peace and prosperity would disappear. The action which God took is detailed in the next chapter.

Chapter Four

Darkness Falls

The Story so Far

In the beginning God created the Heaven and the Earth. That is all the Bible is going to tell you about the original Creation. It will tell you a lot about God, who He is and what He is like but it will not say how He created the universe, how long it has taken Him nor how long ago was the beginning. It will say that the foundation of the Earth was laid in the beginning and that the Earth itself as a planet has developed or evolved. It will also strongly hint that life itself has evolved during those pre-historic ages. We will explain that at a later stage. It is very difficult to calculate years in relation to the Earth since there was no sun by which to measure a day or month or year. The Earth was not part of a solar system throughout those ages.

As it passed through its various stages or ages the Earth would maintain constant daylight and a constant temperature. There was no day or night. Darkness, death and disease are associated with evil and there was no evil in any part of the universe for a very long time.

We have seen how that a spirit of evil entered the scene in Heaven through one of the top angels and ultimately spread to contaminate life on Earth by the appearance of aggressive hostile dinosaurs. These first showed symptoms of disease and then more ferocious breeds began to appear.

God had to come out in judgement or the whole planet and eventually the whole universe would be subject to violence and death.

Now read on:

> *The earth was without form and void and darkness was upon the face of the deep.*

Genesis 1:2

Whereby the world that then was, being overflowed with water, perished.

2 Peter 3:6

Science has established irrefutable evidence that the Earth is millions of years old and that there have been various forms of life on Earth for a very long time. It is undeniable that man in his present form appeared rather less than six thousand years ago.

Science has more recently established that some long time ago a terrible disaster overtook the Earth by which quite suddenly all the dinosaurs perished. It has also proved beyond doubt that the cause of the sudden demise of these creatures was by means of a flood. With this the Bible entirely agrees and says that not only did the dinosaurs perish but that the whole world perished and means that life on this planet was totally destroyed. Thus science and the Bible are not in dispute. The Earth did begin when the Creation began and that at some point in time much more recently life on Earth was brought to an end. Whatever science discovers about life on this planet between the Creation and the disaster, the Bible will not disagree with because it says nothing about it. If they find remains of some primitive evolved form of ape so be it. The Bible does not dispute their findings. The only thing the Bible makes clear is that for most of the time during those ages from the Ice Age onwards, there was no such thing as evil.

So what happened? How did the flood come about? The Bible will not tell us because it is not important to the Bible story. The Bible is about the re-making of the Earth, the appearance of man, his fall and the eventual appearance on Earth of the Son of God to put it right by His death and Resurrection.

The Earth was one continent and one ocean. It is presumed that the one ocean was the Pacific and that the Atlantic did not exist during the early ages of the Earth. Neither did the Mediterranean although there may well have been lakes and rivers. One shelf stretched from Cape Horn to Cape of Good Hope and across to the tip of India and round the coasts of Japan. It would have been possible for animals to travel from California across to China and even Japan. One land mass. How did the level of water in the ocean rise until the whole continent was flooded? You will have to rely solely on scientific evidence.

One theory is that an asteroid hit the Earth and scientists are searching for the massive crater it would have made. But supposing it hit the Earth over the ocean? There would be no crater. A very large asteroid, up to a thousand miles across would hit the atmosphere belt of the Earth which would not be the same as we have now and the bottom of the asteroid would glow with heat and disintegrate on impact. Large meteorite rocks would be thrown off it on to the land. The remainder of the rocky mass would sink to the bottom of the Pacific and remain there until this day. The bed of the Pacific is worth a study. It has always been underwater since the ice melted and has never seen the light of day. I believe that at its deepest point it is about six miles deep. Is there a part where there is a mountain and the summit is within two or three miles of the surface?

This theory is a good one. Most of the sites of drowned dinosaurs appear to be along the west coast of North America from Canada down to Mexico. They support the notion that a huge tidal wave swept over the whole of that coastline. I understand that over four hundred dinosaurs drowned fleeing along a river to escape a massive wall of water and mud. Which way were they facing when they drowned? Also along that stretch of coast are some craters left by meteors. Such a theory would account for the enormous tidal bore and for the level of water in the ocean to rise sufficiently to flood the whole of the continent.

If such an asteroid did hit the Earth it would not be accidental but would be an act of divine intervention. But God as Creator would not need to send an asteroid. He could just as easily send a monsoon type of storm and cause it to rain without ceasing for a hundred years until the whole of the surface of the Earth was under water. It had never rained before and Earth had not experienced any storm or devastation by hurricane or monsoon. If God wanted to destroy life He could do so quite easily by the mother of all storms. The flood in the days of Noah came a long time after and was over within a year. I believe that this disaster was something else altogether. We may never know and never need to know. Suffice it to say that the Bible and science agree that it happened on a massive scale. Our first picture of the Earth is of a planet totally under water, therefore a flood of horrendous proportions must have taken place.

The flood was judgement enough in itself and was capable of destroying all life on Earth except of course the fish in the sea. But worse was to come which would extinguish even such creatures as had evolved and could live in the water. At some point in time we know not whether it was before, during or after the flood, the Earth was plunged into total darkness. All created light had been withdrawn. In short, the Earth had become a dead planet.

Astronomers have found that many radar soundings have gone and been returned from spots where it was thought no star existed. May I put forward the theory that there were many stars in the universe where some form of life existed and that they all suffered the same fate as the Earth? Life was extinguished and the planets plunged into darkness. You see, the Bible states that what we Christians call 'The Plan of Redemption' affects the whole creation and was to be followed through to its logical conclusion on Earth. Stars were contaminated by evil in the shape of death and disease. All evil is to be removed from the body universal by the death and Resurrection and subsequent reign of Jesus Christ. The demise of the dinosaurs made it inevitable that one day the Son of God would be nailed to a cross.

There are two kinds of darkness in the world according to the Bible. One is the darkness where God dwells. You may say that God dwells in light that no man can approach unto. True. But He can turn the light off can He not? God does not have to always reveal the fullness and brightness of His glory! He is intrinsically the invisible spirit and does not always clothe Himself with light. Moses went up into Mount Sinai to the *darkness where God was*. He was not afraid to enter that darkness because he knew that God was there. It is true even today that darkness can enter some of our lives through disability, blindness or bereavement. But many Christians will tell you that in their darkest hour they felt most keenly the presence of God. Such darkness is friendly and comforting because He is there with us. It reminds me of a child that is afraid of the dark, but not when his father is with him holding his hand.

There is the other kind of darkness which is the domain of Satan, the Prince of Darkness. The Earth felt this darkness briefly when the Israelites were in Egypt and in one of the plagues it was dark in Egypt but the Israelites had light in their dwellings. You see God can control the light and the dark. It was an uncomfortable darkness and they were glad to see it removed. The Earth will see this again soon when the trumpets of woe sound in the Book of Revelation. Darkness will cover the Earth, so strong that people we are told will gnaw their tongues in pain. Briefly, for three hours at Calvary the two darknesses of God and Satan met in conflict. God won because the Prince of Darkness met the Lord of Light and lost.

The darkness that fell in Genesis 1:2 was the darkness of evil, being the complete withdrawal of created light. If you could have taken a boat onto the sea then you would have felt the total darkness closed in on you, sinister, menacing with no hint of any sort of light or comfort. You would have been frightened. Dark, foreboding, forbidding spine chilling raw evil would have terrified you. You see God had withdrawn himself from the planet and there was now neither light, life or love there. Satan had it all to himself.

Science is aware that if life disappears on a stretch of stagnant water then the water goes stale and the air goes foul. There being no plants or animals to use the oxygen the balance of nature is disturbed. Hydrogen is released from the water and nitrogen is released from the air. The two get together to form ammonia and the air reeks. It can only get worse when there is no light or life to fight the decay. This is what had happened to the Earth. It became *without form*. The word 'form' does not mean that it had no shape because it had to have a shape of some sort. It means it had no plan or outline, in other words, the Earth had no future plans. It was dead and could only deteriorate. After hundreds, perhaps thousands of years the dinosaurs and the rotting carcasses of dead creatures and the decaying remains of dead plants would emit methane gas in increasing quantities. The planet was dead and could only get worse. It was void, which means it was desolate and empty of all living things. This is our first actual glimpse of Earth. A foul, stinking dead planet reeking of ammonia and every other kind of noxious gas. Death, desolation, darkness and deep waters. Any astronaut passing by would assume that the Earth was incapable of sustaining any kind of life, and he would be right.

Up to this point science and the Bible are in complete agreement. The Bible says that Creation was the work of a great spirit that we call God. Since no other being would have either the knowledge or the power to do so science cannot refute the claim.

Most Bible scholars agree now that there is a massive gap in time between the first two verses of the Bible and that these verses cover all the ages which Science has already discovered existed. During the last century Mr Darwin explored the Galapagos Islands in the South Pacific and worked out that life had evolved on the Earth for millions of years and of course he was right. If my memory serves me correctly he began his book on evolution with an apology. He was not trying to prove that God had nothing to do with Creation. Rather, he was saying to the theologians of his day, 'are you sure you have read your Bibles right?'

There was something of course that Mr Darwin did not know, but later scientists were to discover that the dinosaurs suddenly became extinct. The Bible agrees with this, and adds that so did everything else on the planet. The whole world perished. Now here comes the big question.

If every form of life died, then nothing survived. How then could any form of life on Earth now be connected with what was alive then?

The whole world died, ceased, was destroyed, perished. Therefore nothing could have evolved from it because nothing survived. The death of the dinosaurs means the death of the theory of evolution. Evolution was perfectly correct up to that disaster. After that God had to come to a dead planet and first remake the conditions capable of sustaining life as we know it and then remake the creatures to live on it. He made adjustments to the climatic conditions to introduce new features and then recreated living creatures. Some of the old creatures remained extinct, some were reconstructed in miniature form and some entirely new forms of life introduced to accommodate the entirely new creation, namely a man in his own image. Nothing alive on Earth now can possibly have descended from the pre-historic days because they all perished. To me the scientists have not taken this fact on board while the theologians have not recognised the significance of the gap between verse one and two.

Evolution is both right and wrong. It is right up to the demise of the dinosaurs but everything alive now had to be a new creation. There has not been time in the last few thousand years for anything to evolve. The only version that fits all the known facts is that recorded in Genesis 1.

Chapter Five

Day One – Lights!

And God said; Let there be light and there was light.
Genesis 1:3

I knew a man some years ago who purchased a lovely house with a very large rear garden. He spent a lot of time and money in setting out the garden with lawns, flower beds and borders etc. After several years he had to go abroad, and rented the house to another man who was not interested in gardens. The result was that for three years not even the lawns were cut and the grass grew three feet high. Weeds sprang up with switch grass and rats tails. The poor man would have broken his heart if he could have seen his lovely garden ruined by sheer neglect. You see the new tenant did not share his love of growing plants. This was due to wilful neglect, but sometimes things we have spent years building up are ruined by deliberate vandalism. It is heart breaking witnessing desecration, destruction and wilful damage.

You can imagine how God must have felt! He had spent probably 5,000 million years building a universe of great beauty, full of peace and prosperity. Everything was progressing wonderfully without a cloud in the sky or a weed in the garden. And then His most trusted angel brought in all manner of undesirable things. This was deliberate sabotage of God's world. Plants were now becoming diseased and animals were dying. Some were even killing each other. This was malicious evil. Evil, remember, is the reverse of life. God did not want death or decay in his world but it was now there. Now God must return to this planet from which He had withdrawn all light and life and seek to repair the damage and start his programme of reconstruction renewal and recreation. What is his first step?

The Spirit of God hovered over the face of the waters.

Genesis 1:2

God never panics and nothing ever takes him by surprise. His first action was for the Spirit to come down and assess the damage and see what needed to be done. This is always God's way in dealing with the depredation brought about by Satan. Even in a human life the Spirit first hovers over the soul in darkness and decides what is to be done.

Let me tell you what God does *not* do. He does not throw the thing away and start afresh. While life on Earth was destroyed, the planet itself remained virtually intact. Jeremiah speaks of God as a potter in whose hands the vessel sometimes becomes marred. But He does not throw that vessel away as useless. Rather, He keeps the same piece of clay and makes another vessel out of it (Jeremiah 18:4).

The other thing that God never does is to walk away and accept defeat saying that it is beyond repair and therefore nothing can be done. In Isaiah 42 we read of a God who finds a bruised reed. He can only get a feeble tune out of it but He does not throw it away. A smoking flax may only give a spluttering flame but He does not stamp out the spark and accept that it is useless. Rather, He works on what little spark is there (Isaiah 42:3).

So it is with the world and with your life and mine. God never gives up until He achieves the purpose He has in mind.

The Spirit hovered. The word is used elsewhere in the Bible of an eagle who feels her nest under attack, and so rises and flutters her wings to protect her young and warn any predators to be wary.

The Spirit as we have seen is the breath or wind of God. Thus, the Spirit of God came on the scene and ruffled the surface of the ocean. That should blow away some of the ammonia clouds!

The Spirit of God weighed up the situation and God knows the mind of the Spirit. The decision was taken. What was needed was light. This was not a call for a searchlight to be directed on to the planet so that God could see what he was doing. God can see just as well in the dark as in the light. Light and dark are both alike to him. Paul says (2 Corinthians 5) that God commanded the light to shine *out* of the darkness not into it.

God did not have to send for a light. God *is* the Light. Light is His nature. The invisible God is a Spirit. When He got Him a clothing of light He became the visible God, the Son of God. This then was what the Spirit asked for. He called for the Son of God to come down to the Earth and put on His garments of brilliant light and glory. Now we have the entire Godhead assembled in the darkness on the surface of the waters. Father, Son and Spirit altogether with all their combined power and wisdom. Get ready for the fireworks.

Our trouble when we read the Bible is that we tend to think of things only in terms of what we know today. Therefore, the coming of light at the start of a new day is seen as the silent dawn. So gentle and secretive that we do not know it has happened until we wake up unless we happen to be near a wood where there is a dawn chorus of birds, or a cockerel crowing.

But this breaking of the Earth's first day was nothing like as quiet as that I assure you.

The light of the glory of God is described as seven times brighter than the noonday sun. Light is heat and heat is energy. This light was a massive brilliant explosion of nuclear power over the whole face of the planet. It could be as hot as God wished to make it. It was no place for anyone other than God to be found with its intense light, and the power of the wind blowing in the great heat. This light was the very presence of God himself in all his glory and would be quite irresistible.

God had previously covered the Earth with light without any sun for millions of years. Giving light to a star was routine work to him because he not only is light but he creates light. Thus particles of daylight were trapped around the Earth and have remained there until this day. Without God we would all be groping around in darkness. He put the daylight there. He could have left the daylight there and not allowed any darkness to return but he had taken the irrecoverable decision to allow good and evil to exist side by side for the time being. The light which He thus created above the Earth, He himself called the day. The darkness which he allowed to come back he called the night. Previously there had been continuous light for ages and then continuous darkness after the disaster. Now God is to let them alternate as part of His plan for them to co-exist.

Another mistake that we make is to think of a day as twenty-four hours as it is now. Remember that there was still no sun or moon and day and night had only just been introduced. It follows that the first period of daylight could be as long as God wished and that the first period of darkness could also have been more than twelve hours. It is not heresy to suggest that each day was exactly the same as now.

There are parts of the Earth even today when one day is a whole year with three months summer and nine months in darkness. With no sun around which to rotate there is no way of knowing how long that first day lasted. God *divided* the light from the darkness, which means that God decided how long that period of light was to last and the darkness to return to the Earth. God can do a thousand years work in one day and can make the work of a day last for a thousand years. We do not know how long that first day lasted. What we do know is that it consisted of one period of daylight and one period of darkness. The evening came and the morning came. That was the first day. We can only say what the Book actually says, and try to understand this was the beginning of an entirely new era for the Earth.

The battle between good and evil light and darkness, Christ and Satan had started with a compromise arrangement by which the two were to alternate. At Calvary came the ultimate conflict between the Lord of Light and the Prince of Darkness, who had his head crushed. One day it will break daylight and the darkness will never return. It would have been unthinkable if the reverse could ever happen.

God who creates light also makes children of light. That is what the saints are called. God is the Father of Light and we shall dwell in Heaven with the saints in light. For us it is light and glory all the way.

God wastes neither time nor words. He seems to be in a hurry to get on with His story. One verse of only ten words tells the story of Creation. God then rushes through several thousand million years of the past ages to present a brief picture of the Earth as dead and in darkness. But He immediately shows the Spirit brooding over it like a mother over a sick child. By the third verse He is already introducing the light.

The light will shine like a laser beam through the whole of the Bible. In the Gospels it becomes the Light of the World as the Son of God the very same Creator shines the light of truth and holiness in a world of error and sin. All who follow Him will not walk in darkness but will have the light of life, as He said to an adulteress (John 8:12). Finally the beam of light reaches the end of the Bible story in the last two chapters of Revelation. There we find a whole new world in which there is no night. There is no sun or moon, no sea, no sorrow, no pain and no tears. God will wipe away all tears from their eyes which simply is another way of saying that God will remove all the things that make us cry. That is the triumph of the light. And over the whole of the redesigned universe Jesus will reign through all the many ages still to come and the darkness of evil will never return.

Thus shall be brought to pass the saying;

Death is swallowed up in victory.
O death, where is thy sting? O grave, where is thy
victory?

1 Corinthians 15:54-55

By this means the Bible story ends with the ultimate and total triumph of the light over the darkness, which is completely eliminated for ever. For the moment, we return to our immediate concern which is the manner of the entry of the light into the world.

The light is the appearance on Earth of the presence of God himself in all His power and glory. He is able to control both the light and the heat. He can be a flame that burns in a bush without burning a single twig. He can also be the same flame behind a curtain, and then come out and incinerate two priests without burning the curtain or the brocade and timber of which the tent is made. With God everything is under complete control. Particles of light are now trapped in the air above the Earth thanks to a massive explosion of nuclear energy, the like of which the world has never seen. What happens next will be revealed on day two.

By introducing day and night God made sure that things would be even between them. On 25th March each year there would be exactly twelve hours each. Then for six months the days would gradually grow longer, peaking on 21st June and then reducing until 25th September after which the nights would grow longer until 21st December when things would again creep back to the spring equinox. Thus, over twelve months the amount of time allotted to both day and night would be the same. Eventually, God will bring about the total abolition of darkness and the Earth will revert to its original status of unbroken daylight and that will be permanent.

Chapter Six
Day Two – Making Space

And God said, Let there be a firmament in the midst of the waters, and let it divide the waters from the waters.
And God made the firmament, and divided the waters which were under the firmament from the waters which were above the firmament: and it was so.
And God called the firmament Heaven.   And the evening and the morning were the second day.

Genesis 1:6-8

Daylight after the first period of light and darkness was called day and night. The scene which came into view on that second day was most unpleasant and not in the least conducive to good life. The waters still covered the whole face of the Earth and were, to say the least, dirty. Methane gas still bubbled up from the bed of the ocean and ammonia still made the air foul. Nothing could live in such an environment.

As God looked on the scene it was apparent that what was needed most was some fresh air. He had to find nitrogen to mix with the oxygen which he himself could supply because that was his own breath of life, but first he would have to make a space to fill with it. There was not much point in making breathable air if there was nothing to hold it.

Why you may well ask did He not just wrap it around the Earth like he does now? Stratosphere, ionosphere etc. would make an atmosphere to support all forms of life. The trouble is that to do so would leave the entire surface of the Earth still submersed in muddy waters. Not even fish could live there let alone birds or animals. So He would simply be supplying fresh air with nothing to breathe it in.

Basically then God must make a space. Then He must find the nitrogen to mix with the oxygen to make up the air.

After that He had to find a way to clean up the water so that life could be introduced that could be sustained. To do that He must find hydrogen.

This was indeed a formidable challenge, but not to God. He knew exactly what He was going to do and had the resources to do it. He made it all look quite simple really.

Notice where He was going to make the space. Our Bibles call it the firmament, but it really means just a space. That space would be between the waters. No, He was not going to erect a wall and have waters one side and the other side with a space in between. God was going to lift half of the waters of the ocean up and literally make a space between the waters left down below and the waters lifted above. Quite simple when you know how. Have you ever thought about how God did it?

Was it with a gigantic nuclear explosion that blew some of the water up into the sky so that it somehow defied the law of gravity and stayed there? Possibly, but I very much doubt it.

The easiest way is to convert the water into steam and then convert it back into water. This is what I suggest God did to the extra large ocean which covered the entire surface of the planet. We have seen already that light was introduced on the first day and that such light was the glory of the presence of God. Light and heat are one and the same. With God however, He can decide how much light there needs to be and whether it is to be just light or whether it is also to give off heat. The heat can then be as high as he requires it, even to equal the inside of a nuclear reactor. If heat was needed to boil the waters of the ocean then God could turn it on and this is what I suggest He did.

The light of the first day became hotter and hotter until the whole ocean was literally boiling. Perhaps this is why the mud in which some of the dinosaurs were encased when they died set hard as concrete and had literally to be chipped away to remove their fossilised bones. The water would boil and massive clouds of steam arise. After some twenty or thirty miles it meets the cold air and condenses back into water again. The result is that He was left with a layer of water up above perhaps half a mile or a mile in depth and considerably less water down below. In between was the space which we now call the sky.

The Bible says that there was a sizeable layer of water up there until the days of the flood of Noah. When that deluge came we are told that the windows of Heaven were opened as well as the fountains of the great deep being broken up. The great deep is the Pacific Ocean and floods came up from below. But the windows of Heaven suggest that the waters which had been up there for 1,657 years came down and formed the Atlantic and Indian Oceans which had not been there before.

So that was how it came to pass that a space was formed between the two layers of water. Maybe that is why we call it the ozone layer because at one time it was ocean. Be that as it may we have arrived at a point where the Earth is sealed in a bubble of water. In between the upper and nether layers of water appeared the atmospheric belt of the Earth.

God had to fill it with air. Hydrogen and nitrogen make up ammonia but apply intense heat and they can be split into two separate gases. So while the heat was boiling the water it was also dividing the ammonia into its constituent parts. God can now take the nitrogen and mix it with oxygen and so make the lovely fresh air that we all breathe.

At the same time the hydrogen can be mixed with oxygen to make a big volume of fresh clean water.

God has now killed four birds with one nuclear stone.

He has made a space called the Heaven which contains the blue sky and the clouds.

He has got rid of the ammonia which would by itself kill everything.

He has manufactured lovely fresh air and filled the sky with it and he has made a new ocean with lovely clean fresh water. Not bad for one day's work do you not agree?

If you stop to think about it the best things in life really are free. Daylight, fresh air and clear water. How wonderful to enjoy the sunshine, the open countryside, the seaside, the rivers and lakes whether walking, watching or fishing. God has provided them all free of charge. He insisted on giving us daylight, even if every few hours it gets dark again for a while. We have the summers, even if they do have some rain just when you have your holiday, and the winter will definitely come again soon. But in a sense God is the daylight because He is the light and it is part of his glory. He is the fresh air in a way because He is the breath of life to all His creatures. God gives us richly all things to enjoy.

When you think about the things that God has provided quite freely rejoice at the evidence of the goodness of God. When you accept that God is the Creator you start to worship him not just as the God of all the Earth but as your own personal God whom you wish to please and serve.

At the same time that He gave us a space filled with breathable fresh air, He also gave the fallen angel Lucifer a temporary home. He was thrown out of Heaven and not allowed to live there. He will not take up residence on Earth until he takes possession of the dead body of the Anti-Christ. Meantime Satan is the Prince of the Power of the Air. He is therefore free to roam the skies above the Earth and through His kingdom of evil spirits assert his evil influence over events on Earth. But that as they say is another story. For the moment we can enjoy the goodness of God and put up with the evil things that God chooses to allow into our lives. They will one day be withdrawn and love, joy and peace will win. I am so glad that we are on the winning side because we belong to Jesus Christ.

God called the Space which He had made, Heaven, but we call it the sky. We will have a few thoughts in a moment about why He called it Heaven when he already had a large Heaven. The more familiar name to us is the sky. It is in fact a mirror of life as we know it and is a miniature Bible to those who do not read the real thing. With all its changing moods and faces the sky is a picture of the tug of war going on between the good and the bad. It brings us sunshine as well as storms and we know that when the skies are grey and foreboding the clouds are ultimately bound to roll by and the sun come out again. The skies therefore are full of hope of better days to come.

There is a saying that the sun always shines on the righteous but this is not what the Bible says. God sends his sunshine on both just and the unjust. That is to say He blesses those who do not deserve it just as easily as those who are worth blessing. You see the goodness of God leads many to repentance by convincing them that God is good. The skies bring days of sunshine as days of rain that are equally days of blessing. At times we need the rain and it does the gardens good. When the sun comes out it is like a tonic to us and we soon forget the dark winter nights. There are days of storm and havoc when it seems evil is uppermost and a lot of damage is done. I suppose that over the year the good days and the bad ones come out about equal. In the sunshine we actually think sometimes that God is smiling on us and purposely sends a little sunshine into our lives as a relief from the gloom. Why did He call it Heaven? Perhaps because God wants us to have a little bit of heaven on Earth and not think that He and his Heaven are millions of miles away.

I know that we occasionally speak of someone being in the seventh heaven of delight but actually the Bible only speaks of three Heavens. There was once a pattern of things in the Heavens. Moses was told to build a tent for God to live in the wilderness of Sinai. He called it the tabernacle and it was built in three parts. First there was an outer court which everyone could see from the gate. Then there was a sanctuary called the Holy Place which only the priests could enter and right inside there was the inner sanctum called the holy of holies where the Ark and Mercy Seat rested like a throne for the Shekinah glory of God. This is described in Hebrews 9 as a pattern of things in the Heavens.

We have the Heaven which we can all see and which we call the sky. Then we have the Heavens which are the many galaxies and constellations plus the Milky Way. There are probably millions of solar systems which we have not seen yet. And finally there is the Heaven of Heavens where the Bible says that God lives. It is the holy of holies of the universe. It is into this Heaven of heavens that Jesus returned after His Resurrection to enter as a man who had died and risen again into the presence of the Most High God.

Solomon, when he prayed at the dedication of his temple, spoke of the Heaven of heavens as not big enough to hold God much less the house that he had built. The entire universe is not big enough to hold God who would fill it all if it were ten times as big. Where is this Heaven of heavens? Is it a layer of stars above those that we can see or is it a constellation like Orion at the centre of the universe? We just do not know but the pattern suggests that it is at the centre with the twelve signs of the Zodiac camped like the twelve tribes of Israel all around it. One thing is certain. God wants us to know that He is not far away and that a little bit of heaven is within our sight.

Chapter Seven

Day Three – Land Ahoy!

And God said, Let the waters be gathered unto one place, and let the dry land appear: and it was so. And God called the dry land Earth; and the gathering of the waters called the Seas: and God saw that it was good.

Genesis 1:9-10

Morning has broken on the third day and already God's programme of reconstruction is two thirds finished and well on schedule for completion on time. Looking below the canopy of water that is above the sky, God can now see a belt of fresh breathable air capable of sustaining any kind of life.

The waters below although now clear are still in turmoil. But compared with the boiling cauldron and nuclear fireworks of the two previous days an observer would describe it as positively placid.

He would however see only the sea and no trace of land. This could provide a wonderful habitat for all kinds of aquatic life including fishes and turtles and such birds as ducks who could live entirely on the water. Beneath the surface of the ocean lie the remains of the lost world of yesteryear and the graveyard of the dinosaurs. God has no intention of making the Earth into one vast aquarium. He has one great ambition, and that is to find a home for His ultimate creation, namely man in his own image. To achieve this He needs to restore the land.

Once again, God does not have to actually do anything. He needs only to speak the Word. Never underestimate the power of the spoken Word of God. It is quite irresistible.

God speaks to the waters which are entirely under His control. The sea is His and He made it says one of the Psalms (95:5). His word of command is, 'let the waters be gathered together into one place'. God had a map in His mind. He had a plan to work to like any builder or landscape gardener. He knew exactly where the sea would end and the land begin. God would set boundaries and there would the proud waves of the sea be stayed. They might over the centuries encroach as at Bedruthan Steps in Cornwall but the boundaries of ocean and land are not substantially altered in a thousand years.

Psalm 104 graphically describes the whole story of Creation and of how God provided for all creatures including man who would subsequently appear on the dry land. Just listen to these most dramatic words:

> *Thou coverest it with the deep as with a garment: the*
> *waters stood above the mountains.*
> *At thy rebuke they fled; at the voice of thy thunder they*
> *hasted away.*
> *They go up by the mountains; they go down by the*
> *valleys unto the place which thou hast founded for them.*
> *Thou hast set a boundary that they may not pass over;*
> *that they turn not again to cover the earth.*
>
> Psalm 104:6-9

What a vivid description of the storm the wind and the thunder by which God ordered the sea to go back and it obeyed! Jesus stilling the waves on Lake Galilee was child's play. He ordered the waves to recede with no more difficulty than you or I might blow the water off a covering sheet of tarpaulin. Cascading down the sides of Himalayas and Alps as well as Andes and Rockies. Up the hills of lesser ranges and down into the valleys. Still the waters raced on as ordered by their Master and Lord until they reached their appointed boundaries beyond which they must not return.

Thus is portrayed the almighty power of the Living God who is Lord of all the Earth. The Pacific Ocean had been reconstructed and would stay like it for the foreseeable future.

So much truth is packed into a word in the Bible! God had said Let the *dry* land appear. But it had been under water for thousands of years. How could it possibly be dry within a day? It is one of those unnoticed miracles for which the Bible is famous. Remember when the Israelites passed through the Red Sea? They went through on *dry land*. With God nothing is impossible.

God has now restored the Earth to the same position it was in just before the disaster. One land mass and one ocean. Whether the land mass was the same as before or smaller or greater we have no way of knowing nor is it of any importance. We do not know its size and shape previously.

The thinking mind will enquire whether it is feasible to believe that God could produce the one Continent in half a day. It is a sensible question and requires a sensible answer. In fact it has two answers. First, as we have already seen it is impossible to measure a day without a sun around which the Earth was to rotate. As we shall see tomorrow the sun was provided partly to calculate days months and years. Therefore there is no way of measuring how long a period of daylight and darkness lasted at this point in time.

It could well have been as long as a year now. That is not to say that God could not do it in twelve hours, but the text does not require us to believe in six days of twenty four hours each as now.

Secondly, Peter speaks of a day being a thousand years and a thousand years as a day. Moses however in his prayer in Psalm 90 says that a thousand years could pass not in one day or even half a day but as a watch in the night. A watch in the night as any seaman will tell you is only three hours. Thus, being God, He could do the work of a thousand years in three hours. God is not tied to time like us. Time is of no significance to Him who belongs to eternity.

A few years ago just off the coast of Iceland a submarine volcanic eruption resulted in the birth of a new island. We watched it on television being born in just two weeks. Within a year there was grass growing on it. That is nature in the hands of God.

It is also not accidental that the re-emergence of Earth took place on the third day. In the Bible the third day usually has a link with Resurrection. The Earth is seen rising like a phoenix from its watery grave after the severe judgement of the Almighty. This is just how God meant it to look. The Earth coming out of the darkness to a new and wonderful life. That is Resurrection.

Notice also that God called the dry land Earth. Have you realised that God never names the Planet? It is only the soil, the rocks, the dry land that he calls Earth.

Commonplace things like Day and Night, Sky, Earth and Sea have been brought into being at the command of God and He has named them. He has separated the day from the night and the waters above the sky from the waters below and the Earth from the sea. That is calculated provision for man. This is not just Nature this is a keen mind at work.

God has reached the point where He has rocks and possibly rivers but there is nothing alive on the planet. He must do something about that very quickly. Soon the land will be crawling with cattle and sheep and many other living creatures. They will need something to eat. And so like a good landlord He is going to stock up the larder for his guests. The food that He ordered to appear was in three parts. There was grass, herbs and trees. Read the words as they appear.

> *And God said, Let the earth bring forth grass, the herb yielding seed, and the fruit tree yielding fruit after his kind, whose seed is in itself on the earth: and it was so.*
>
> *And the earth brought forth grass, and herb yielding seed after its kind, and the tree yielding fruit after its kind, whose seed was in itself, after its kind: and God saw that it was good.*

Genesis 1:11-12.

Is not the language majestic in its simplicity? No earthly author would have passed over so important a development in such few words but God is eager to get on with the job.

The first sign of actual life on the Earth was that grass began to spring up all over the place. The wording used is 'tender grass'. Exactly the same word as used by David in Psalm 23. He makes me to lie down in green pastures. Pastures of tender grass. All over the world new shoots of tender grass were springing up. The cynic will say that this is natural in the hot house that was the Earth then for out of the caked mud that had been under water for thousands of years there would be sure to be grass springing up. The miracle is repeated every spring after the snows and cold of winter the Earth bursts out into new life and grass grows where we thought the land was dead.

Grass is very good. Not only will the cows and goats that will soon come be able to eat it, but when it is mixed with the fluid secretions in their stomachs it will produce milk for their young and the young of humans. Not only is it very good for food but if a child falls down it will not be hurt if it falls on grass, for grass is very gentle. Ask any footballer whether he would rather play on grass than on plastic. Moreover grass is very restful to the eyes. The more I think about it the more grateful I am that God introduced grass on to the planet. It grows in the sand dune and it grows in the fields after the harvest has been reaped and it seems to grow entirely by itself without any help from man.

The more it rains the faster it grows. And often among it grow all manner of wild flowers which no one ever planted there. This is the goodness of God for our benefit.

Next, God ordered a quantity of herbs. Now once again we must put out of our minds the normal picture of herbs as being a limited group of plants such as thyme, sage, parsley, rosemary, basil, mint and so on. These to us have great healing powers, more perhaps than most of us know, but in cooking they are for seasoning and flavouring, not the main substance of the meal. God said later in the chapter that the herbs were given for food to the animals and to man. We therefore have a wide range of food products suitable for both animals and humans. Root crops and vegetables and small plants such as tomatoes. The key phrase used is 'after its kind'. God did not overnight produce every conceivable kind of vegetable but he introduced each basic species from which man has cross bred and propagated many other kinds. Chapter 1 of Genesis tells us what God did, while Chapter 2 tells us a little of how He did it. Let us quote again the words of the Lord.

And the Lord God made...every plant of the field before
it was in the earth, and every herb of the field before it
grew.

Genesis 2:5

So there you have it. God actually made each original species of herb and plant and planted them out. He seems to have continued to make them and bring them to Adam to plant out before sin came in.

A whole range of plants, herbs and shrubs primarily for food many of which were brand new and had not been seen before were made.

God had man in mind when he brought about the great re creation of the Earth. Things were put in for his benefit and for him to look after.

Ultimately on this third day God turned to the making of trees. As we have seen there is no evidence of any large scale forestation on Earth during the days of the dinosaurs or I am sure scientists would have discovered it. There was a lot of foliage. I saw on television recently that scientists have discovered some trees in Australia which they think are pine trees from pre-historic days. I would be very interested to know if these could have survived under two or three miles of salt water for several thousand years. Have they been fossilised?

Now there must be trees. God mentions specifically the fruit trees which require man to cultivate. The two key phrases are 'after its kind' and 'whose seed is in itself'. God appears to have made each kind of tree. Citrus fruits and hard fruits such as apples. Soft fruits such as bananas. Such things as melons and yams would be among the plants. Each orange tree could produce a hundred oranges and inside each orange could be five pips which when planted out could in theory grow into another five hundred orange trees. Five hundred trees could within a few years come from one original tree. This was to be the job of Adam to replenish the Earth and subdue it. Put the seed back into the Earth and stop it growing too fast.

Man would also require wood trees, that is trees just for the timber. Man would be required to cut the tree down in time in order to make furniture, houses, ploughs and so on. Oak trees, cedar trees, pine trees would be needed. They were probably not there before man. God would also provide trees just to remain green all the year round and make the hillsides and valleys look so beautiful. God loves beauty and colour. How did He make the trees? Well again in the second chapter we are told that God caused the trees to grow out of the ground. That is to say that He made a living tree and planted it so that it would start to grow. No man is capable of making a living tree. Man cannot even make a single daffodil bulb so that when planted it will grow. It has to be alive.

Let us not think that overnight the Earth was covered in pine forests and leafy glades. God was starting with basic species manufactured by himself alive and planted out. In some cases the wind and the birds would carry seeds to other regions of the Earth and they would be self planted. That is how the rain forests came to be formed. Man appears to have had no hand except to chop them down. God in His infinite wisdom planned the entire Earth eventually to be cultivated with grass, shrubs and trees. Enough to meet the needs of every living creature on the planet.

As we have said God is a conservationist and here He was in His element. He loves growing things and living things and with the entire surface of the land to play with, He landscaped it into a thing of unrivalled beauty.

Where can you find greater beauty than in the lofty snow capped peaks and pine clad slopes of the Rockies? There are the fjords of Norway and the great sweeps of the Mississippi and other rivers. No human hand has been involved, yet they take one's breath away with their splendour. Let us not fail to give God the glory for that which He has done.

Chapter Eight

Day Four – Central Heating Installed

And God said, Let there be lights in the firmament of the heaven to divide the day from the night; and let them be for signs, and for seasons, and for days and years: And let them be for lights in the firmament of the heaven to give light upon the earth: and it was so.

And God made two great lights; the greater light to rule the day, and the lesser light to rule the night: He made the stars also.

Genesis 1:14-16

God has now reached the halfway stage in his massive programme of reconstruction. Three days down and three to go. He has a recognisable planet with vegetation growing on it but nothing else. What he needs is a constant and controllable supply of heat.

During the pre-historic ages there was always light, but the temperature started at below zero during the Ice Age and very slowly moved upwards. The heat was only what was required. There were no hot house plants growing and the dinosaurs when they finally arrived on the scene were hardly likely to go sunbathing on the beach. The temperature therefore would be low but increasing to mild as needed. God is able to supply both light and heat. That is His nature. Now however he arrives at a most important decision. He will have a great light in the sky to give heat as much or as little as required. He will also have a smaller light to shine during the night. He is in fact going to create a sun and a moon.

When I was at school a very long time ago I seem to remember being told that long ago a gentleman named Copernicus startled the egg-heads of his time by announcing that in his opinion the Earth was not flat but round. Moreover, he said that it was not the centre of the universe and that the sun did not rotate around the Earth as commonly taught. Of course some doubtless argued with him at the time but soon realised that he was right. The Earth is a global sphere even if not exactly circular in shape. The Earth does travel round the sun and it takes a year to do so. The sun may not be the centre of the whole universe but it is the centre of our solar system.

From these true facts other conclusions have been drawn. It is thought that the Earth came off our sun as did all of the stars in our solar system. The sun therefore must be older than them all and have been created first. From time to time huge balls of fire have been flung and have cooled down to form all the planets that make up our solar system.

It is surprising to notice that the Bible has always set out a totally different story. The sun was not made until the fourth day of Creation therefore it is the Earth that is older than the sun and it cannot possibly have come off our existing sun. This is not a theory but a stated Biblical fact. Since it cuts right across current thinking we have to examine it very closely to see whether the statement has been misunderstood or whether another explanation has to be found.

In the Book of Acts Chapter 7 Stephen, the first Christian martyr, makes his final speech to his accusers before being dragged out to be stoned to death. He relates the history of the Jewish nation from Abraham to David. When he comes to the part played by Moses he tells how Moses went up into the holy mount (Sinai) and received the living Oracles. Six weeks he spent up there face to face with God and received the Law and the details of how to construct the tabernacle for God to live in among his people. At the same time God dictated to him the contents of Genesis. All faithful Jews like all Christians have always believed that the writing of Genesis was done by Moses but the words were the words of God. In this Jews and Christians are in total agreement. These are sacred writings. Divinely inspired as Moses was moved by God Himself. We would therefore be very ill advised to ignore the Creator's own account of what He did and how He did it.

On this fourth day God does not go into detail as to how He made the sun and moon. He simply says that He made them. For a creator to manufacture a ball of fire that makes its own combustible material is not difficult to accept. Science may discover how the sun manages to make its own fuel. Sufficient to take on face value God's own claim that he made the sun and the moon on the fourth day.

If He does not describe how He did it, because He does not have to, God does tell us why He did it. Firstly, to establish the clear division between day and night. Let it divide the light from the darkness. Now He had said this on the first day when He brought in the light. Now He is going to strengthen that division. By bringing in a sun He is introducing a light that is brighter than the daylight. It is not there to cause the daylight but to dominate it. Each morning the sun will rise and each evening the sun will set. It will continue its journey through the sky every day and return the next day. It will soon establish a fixed orbital path moving from the Tropic of Cancer to the Tropic of Capricorn on either side of the Equator and so sharing its warmth over a wide band of the surface of the Earth.

At the same time he will make a smaller light to dominate the night. Darkness in Scripture will always speak of the domain of Satan but he is not going to have complete freedom of the night hours. A moon would be put in so that a good degree of light would shine even in the darkness of the night to help any man who has to travel or work, and to help those animals who go out to look for food under cover of darkness. They could be in serious danger if they ventured out in daylight. So the moon will wax and wane three weeks out of every four, and only in one week in every four will the Earth be in total darkness, except for whatever light comes from the stars, clouds permitting.

This is not only practical but also highly symbolic. The sun and moon are there God says for signs, for seasons, for days and for years. So they serve a very real purpose and tell us many truths.

They are for signs. These signs have nothing to do with the signs of the Zodiac nor with horoscopes and astrology. The Bible looks with great disfavour on telling the future by means of stars, palm reading or cards or anything else. It is dismissed as being the work of demons and not of God. If God wants us to know what is going to happen he will tell us if he wants to. If it is bad I personally would rather not know. And if it is good then it will be a very pleasant surprise if I was not expecting it. Trust God I say.

The sun and moon however are there for signs. I would like to suggest that the sun is a sign in at least four ways.

Firstly, it is a *sign of God's glory*. While the sun is brighter than the daylight, there is a light that is brighter than the sun. Peter, James and John saw it on the Mount of Transfiguration. The raiment of Jesus became white and glistering and his countenance or face was like the sun shining in its strength. One describes it as seven times brighter than the noonday sun. That is only a faint glimpse of the glory of God in the face of Jesus Christ his Son.

When Saul of Tarsus met Jesus on the Damascus Road he was stricken with blindness because he saw a light above the brightness of noonday sun. The Eternal Son is clothed with the brightness of his Father's glory and that light is many times brighter than the sun in its strength. Thus the sun at its height reminds me personally of the glory of God, that is so bright angels have to veil their faces and no man could dare look at it.

Secondly, the sun is a *sign of the goodness of God.* It germinates the crops and ripens the grain. It shines on the just and on the unjust so that God is good to all, even to those who do not deserve it. The sun cheers us up when we are feeling down in the dumps. When we are lying on the beach soaking up the sunshine it is very easy to believe that God is in His Heaven and all is right with the world. And although life is very much a mixture of good and evil, there is no doubt that God is good. Listen to what James, who was the half brother of Jesus and brought up with Him in the same house from birth, has to say.

Every good gift, and perfect gift comes from above,
and comes down from the Father of lights, with whom
nothing varies, and nothing turns aside.

James 1:17

Yes, we are very grateful for the sunshine even if we do not always get it when we want it. They say that it is better than a bottle of medicine in helping us to forget our troubles.

Thirdly, the sun is a *sign of the greatness of God.* Who else could start a fire that would keep on stoking itself up without ever having to put more coal on? The nearest that man gets to it is with a fire that is connected to an endless supply of electricity or gas or oil. But man has to make a power station to feed all the electric fires. God needs to do no such thing. When you enjoy the sunshine remember the Psalm that says, 'Ascribe ye greatness to our God'. When you think that God put that fire ninety three million miles from the Earth and yet at times its heat is unbearable you glimpse a little of the greatness of our God. Such accuracy of location is greater than any man could arrange. The scientists find a keyhole in the sky and put a satellite into orbit at the exact height needed to remain in station at the same point above the Earth and we think that is marvellous. How much more the skill and power of our great God.

The moon is a reflector of the light of the sun and has no light of its own. The moon is a *sign of the grace of God*. God is by nature very loving and very gracious. Even when we have to have darkness there is a mirror that reflects the light of God and lightens our darkness. Man is normally expected to work during the daylight and sleep during the night restoring the energies that he has used. But some people have to go out to work during the hours of darkness, and sailors and others have to travel when there is no artificial light such as street lamps. God has kindly given thought to their needs. We have to have darkness simply because God has decreed that some part of the time must be given to the powers of darkness under the control of Satan. And so we do get adversity in our lives. Illness, bereavement, war and strife. But it seems to me that in every time of evil some good emerges. Acts of heroism and bravery and unselfishness are often seen during times of great misery. People who become physically handicapped often find resources of strength that they did not know that they possessed. Paul had a thorn in the flesh. It was some physical drawback that he three times asked God to take away so that he could serve him better. When he realised that God had put it there for a purpose, he thanked God for it and accepted that when he was weak that was really when he was strongest. God said *My grace is sufficient for you*. He was weak so that the power of Christ could rest upon him. The moon was reflecting the light of the sun. The light of Christ was shining on him in the darkness.

The sun and moon however, we must remember, are only temporary measures. They were not there previously as they were not needed. The time will come when they will be removed. The time is coming very soon when Jesus Christ will return to Earth to reign over it in peace and prosperity for a thousand years. Satan is physically bound in the bottomless pit and cannot interfere. That is the only way to deal with an evil spirit. Lock him up. When he is released he will again try to prove that there is a better way than God's way of honesty, holiness and love, and some people will actually believe him. He will form an army and there will be a short war against Jesus which will be over very quickly. The Earth will then be destroyed by fire along with certain other planets and will be replaced by a new Heaven and a new Earth. That Earth will have neither sun nor moon because the glory of God and of the Lamb will give it all the light and all the heat it needs. Read all about it in Revelations 20-22. This means that the sun and moon will have been in operation for about seven thousand years and after that they will be redundant.

Which leads us to the final question regarding the sun. The Earth is obviously a lot older than the sun in fact we have already seen that it is probably as old as any other star in the universe and has been there in some form or other from the beginning of Creation. Obviously then the Earth did not come off our existing sun. In that case we must ask where it did come from. If as science believes it started its life from some nebula such as the one in Orion then it has had a very long journey through deep space before finding its present position in the Milky Way. This very long journey would account for the fact that in the absolute zero of outer space it would be frozen like a giant ice roll for millions of years.

In Isaiah 40 we are told of God 'stretching out the heavens like a curtain'. This supports the scientific theory of a Big Bang. It may well be that a lot of stars were thrown off the Nebula like stars from a Catherine Wheel. Eventually a vast explosion scattered them to all parts of the universe. On the other hand one great big star could have exploded into a million parts and they all be scattered like grapeshot. There is no way of knowing. It is not important to the Bible story.

If the Earth started its life in Orion it would take millions of years at the speed of light to reach the Milky Way. Many changes would take place and the sheer friction on its journey would cause the slight changes of temperatures the planet evolved and life evolved upon it. It would travel as an independent planet and not part of any solar system.

Finally, it reaches the end of its long journey through space and joins a host of stars in the Milky Way. Genesis 1 says specifically that on the fourth day God made the sun and the moon. I believe that to be a true statement. It is possible that they were already there like the saying Here is one I made earlier. The Earth would join a sun that had been previously made but I think that that is bending Scriptural interpretation. *No.* I think that on the fourth day God actually made these two great lights and that they would last only for seven thousand years and will then be destroyed. Seven thousand years is a mere hiccup. A bleep on the screen of time between five billion years previously and an unending eternity to come.

There are many things in the world around us that remind me of verses in the Bible. The sun reminds me of a couple of verses in Malachi.

For, behold, the day comes, that will burn as an oven; and all the proud, yea, and all that do wickedly shall be stubble...saith the Lord of hosts...But unto you that fear my name shall the Sun of righteousness arise with healing in his wings.

Malachi 4:1-2

But you might say what about the other stars in our system? Does it not say that he made the stars also? Surely Venus, Jupiter and the others are more than six thousand years old. I quite agree but here we come to correct Scriptural interpretation. We have to note exactly what is said.

The words 'he made' in our English text are in italics. Now in normal English prose words in italics have extra importance. In the Bible however the opposite is true. Italics mean that the words were not there in the original Hebrew and that the translators put them in to make what they considered to be sense. If we miss them out we read 'The stars also'. He made the sun and the moon on the fourth day and the stars were also there. This leads to the idea that when He made the sun and moon, the Earth and the other members of our solar system were drawn into orbit around the newly made sun, and so a new solar system was created by making the sun last and not first. This is what I suggest happened. Once again it would take a little time for the Earth to be drawn into its present orbital path so that a day would still be a little longer than twenty-four hours.

Chapter Nine

Day Five – Stocking the Aquarium and the Aviary

And God said, Let the waters bring forth abundantly the moving creature that hath life, and fowl that may fly above the earth in the open firmament of heaven.
And God created great whales, and every living creature that moveth, which the waters brought forth abundantly after their kind, and every winged fowl after his kind: and God saw that it was good.
And God blessed them, saying, be fruitful, and multiply, and fill the waters in the seas, and let fowl multiply in the earth.
And the evening and the morning were the fifth day.

Genesis 1:20-23

Some four or five years ago I was invited to give the first talk in a series looking at the character of God as depicted in the various names and titles given to him in the Old Testament.

There are four main names and in order to distinguish them to the ordinary reader they are usually printed in different lettering in our Authorised Version.

GOD in all capitals normally means *El* the Almighty, and speaks of His great power.

God spelt with a capital G means *Elohim* the Creator and as we have previously seen is the plural of *El* and really means *Almighty Ones*. The Creator is thus all three members of the Godhead.

LORD in all capitals is *Jehovah* and is the *Great I Am,* the Covenant Maker, and has always to do with salvation.

Lord spelt with a capital L is *Adonia* and means the sovereign Lord or King, and speaks of His majesty and authority.

I started the series with a talk on God the Creator, and His name *Elohim* from the first chapter of Genesis.

The first thing that I noticed in this chapter was the constant repetition of the word 'and'. To be candid, I think that we are meant to notice it. It is a figure of speech called 'emphasis by repetition'. It is knocking a nail on the head several times in order to drive it in firmly. To change the metaphor it reminds one of piling brick upon brick in order to build a wall.

And God said, Let there be light

And there was light.

And God saw the light that it was good

And God divided the light from the darkness

And God called the light day

And the darkness he called night;

And the evening and the morning were the first day.

And so it goes on all the way down the chapter. At school I was taught never to begin a sentence with a preposition and yet here was the Bible breaking the first rule of grammar. But in my boyhood mind it made the Bible stand out as superior to the normal rules employed by a normal writer.

The next thing that I noticed when reading through the chapter to prepare for the talk was that while Genesis is supposed to be the great chapter on Creation the word 'create' comes in the first verse and then is not used again until the fifth day. This struck me as being very curious.

We humans think of the breaking forth of the light and the making of the firmament and the emergence of the Earth and sea and making of plants and trees as all being acts of creation. But God does not call them creative acts. So we ask what does God consider to be an act of creation?

The word for 'create' is an extension of the verb 'to be' and simply means 'to cause to come into being' or to bring into existence.

The true Creator first creates something out of nothing. If He makes a thing out of nothing then He must first make the materials with which to do the making. God started with empty space as we saw in Chapter 1. Clothed with light he has the energy to make anything he chooses. He can produce electrons, protons and neutrons with which to build any molecular atomic structure he wishes. He can make any gas He needs. After all, where else can He find the materials with which to build a universe? He is the only true creator because He begins with nothing but Himself and His own power and knowledge.

Secondly, the Creator must have a purpose in mind. God has to have a reason for everything He does. He is not interested in ornamentation or adornment. God is practical and purposeful. That is why He knew what He had in mind when He made planet Earth and He will always achieve his purposes.

Thirdly, the Creator must be able to see the whole thing through from start to finish. As this involves many hundreds of thousands of years this aspect alone is beyond the reach of mortal man. When a man starts a business he may leave instructions as to how he wants it conducted after his death but it will in the very nature of things be left to his successor to see that those instructions are carried out. God has no successor and is able to supervise the whole of His creation from everlasting to everlasting. He is God. From the ages that have now ceased to the ages that are yet to come God is working his purposes out. There will be difficulties and setbacks on the way but God will never be deflected from his goal.

Fourthly, the Creator is more than the creator of the material universe. The God of Abraham is the creator of Abraham; God created the man of faith and gave him the faith to use. Man is never born with faith. His life was shaped by the guiding hand of his creator.

The God of Israel is the creator of the nation of Israel. He has plans for the nation and all his promises to Abraham, Isaac, Jacob, Moses and David will be kept. They include the coming of a Messiah and Millennium reign of Christ.

God is the creator of every Christian, because according to Ephesians 2 we are his workmanship created in Christ Jesus. If any man be in Christ he is a new creation says Paul (2 Corinthians 5). So while the Church is the Body of Christ and is also created by God, the wonderful truth is that every individual Christian is a separate act of creation from His hands. He calls them all by names, links Isaiah 40 with the creation of the stars and the calling of the sheep in John 10.

To create, then, is to make something absolutely new, out of nothing and to follow it through right into eternity.

God created the universe in verse one but when He called for the light He does not consider that He created anything. He merely brought the light that was there, namely His own presence and glory and caused it to burst upon the darkness that covered the Earth.

When He called for a space between the waters above and the waters below, once again He was not creating anything new. He was merely making a space to fill with breathable air.

When the Earth emerged from the ocean God simply ordered the water to retreat and the land to re-appear. Not an act of creation in the mind of God although we would have called it that. God just ordered the surface of the Earth to come into view once more.

Then He made the grass to grow, the herbs, plants and trees to appear. Surprisingly, God only says that He commanded the Earth to bring forth grass etc. He made the plants and trees and planted them to grow. God says that that is making things that are rooted in the ground and can only grow so long as they remain rooted. That is not creation says God.

When on the fourth day He made the sun and the moon He still does not think that He has created anything new. He must by then have millions of suns and millions of solar systems. Making one more was nothing new to Him, in fact it was routine. He had a sky full of them. It is not until we come to the fifth day that we learn the last essential thing about a creative act. It must be a living thing that moved about. These would be living creatures.

God is now confronted by the greatest challenge to both his desire and His ability to create living things. It is a challenge which He will meet head on gladly because it gives Him the opportunity to do what He most enjoys doing, namely making living things. Before Him is a giant pool. Five thousand miles across from east to west and at least five thousand miles from north to south. We call it the Pacific Ocean. The temperature has now dropped to near normality from its furnace heat of four days ago. The water is clean and fresh, but it is completely empty. The task confronting the Creator is to fill it with living creatures.

Over many millions of years life has evolved from one basic original form of life which God himself had introduced. As we have seen, that life had to be destroyed. Now he must replace it. He can, of course, leave it to evolve all over again for a few more hundreds of millions of years but the trouble with that idea is that it will again end in failure. Sooner or later he would arrive at the same point where he would have to destroy it again. It is a fact of life that if you do something and it goes wrong and you simply do it again the same way then it will go wrong again. God has to approach the problem from another angle with a permanent solution in mind so instead of allowing it to evolve again, He is going to create it all in one day with some important additions. We will think more about that in the next two chapters when he introduces animals and then man. God has known all along that the only solution to a spiritual problem is a spiritual solution. He now embarks on the plan to send His Son to Calvary as a human sacrifice for sin which solution He saw before the foundation of the world according to Peter (1 Peter 1:19-20).

In creating fishes we see three factors. He is thinking of created beings that will live in or on the water and will depend on the water for their survival. As any marine biologist will tell you, the world below the surface is a totally different and wonderful world to that which we know personally. The other day I saw on television some pictures taken deep down on the bed of the Pacific. A camera was lowered to take still photos at regular intervals. Remember that the Pacific has always been under water since the ice melted. Life on Earth began in the Pacific millions of years ago. This camera showed that there is a creature or creatures actually alive in the mud because the mud kept moving, and occasionally spine-like fins emerged but not a head above the mud. Can there be creatures that actually survived the disaster? Earlier films taken about two miles down show ghost-like creatures with pale bodies that have never seen the light of day and never been within two miles of the surface. What little do we know of the bed of the Pacific.

To return to Genesis 1 we learn first of the *will of God*.

'And God said, Let the waters bring forth *abundantly*.' Now there is a word that delights the heart of God. He is a God of abundance. Why settle for a lit

When Jesus (John 6) was thinking of feeding the five thousand families, the disciples thought only of every one having a little in order to keep them going till they got home. But Jesus was thinking of every one being filled and going home satisfied. That is the God we deal with. A God of abundance.

Secondly, we think of the *works of God*. And God created great whales and every living thing that moves in the waters. Evolution started with the little plankton and micro organisms then moved on to crustaceans and so upwards. God seems in Creation to begin with the large sea creatures. Whales actually means all large sea monsters as they were called including sharks and manta rays. 'Great' in Hebrew means great in number as well as great in size. God begins with the large ones but they have to have plankton and krill to eat. Whales are not predators except for one species as I understand it. They are gentle giants and feed on the smallest creatures. Perhaps the thought is that God was providing creatures that would be peaceful and pleasant as opposed to those whose very nature is to prey on other fishes.

I do not know if there had been any whales before but God put them there now and created them for His own pleasure.

He also introduced a whole range of fishes from cod, bass, whiting, mackerel and so on as food for man who was shortly to come. These are created beings for the benefit of mankind.

Thirdly, we notice the *ways of the Lord*. And God blessed them and said to them be fruitful and multiply. The same blessing that he was going to bestow on man. God's ways are ways of blessing. It would be wrong to think that the Creator made millions of fish swimming around by the end of the fifth day. He needed only to create a breeding pair of whales or cod and nature would do the rest in time. God creates and then blesses. Multiplication is one form of divine blessing.

And so from whales to whelks, from sharks to shrimps, from manta ray to mussels, from bass to barnacles – God enjoys his favourite pastime of creating. Every possible size, shape, colour and type of creature he made and introduced them to the water.

These included seals and turtles as well as anemones and jelly fish. You name it and God thought about it and made it. Each one was alive and could immediately start spawning or breeding. That is the glory of the Creator.

God hates empty spaces and so He thought of the skies above the surface of the Earth and of the sea. He began at once to create species of flying fowl. Gulls and tern that could live on the water and extract their food from the fishes. Birds on the land of every conceivable colour and make. The nature films that we see on television tell us a lot about the photographer and his or her patience and skill. But they tell of the glory of the God who created all things and they were created for His pleasure. And of course God could go on making things for a long time after the fifth day. Each after its kind is the phrase. God introducing basic species of sea creature and flying birds. They only could come from the hand of God because there is no time for anything to evolve. But we see a lot more of the glory of God on the sixth day.

Chapter Ten
Day Six (Part 1) – Bring on the Animals

And God said, Let the earth bring forth the living creature after his kind, cattle and creeping thing, and beast of the earth after his kind: and it was so.
And God made the beast of the earth after his kind, and cattle after their kind, and every thing that creepeth upon the earth after his kind: and God saw that it was good.

Genesis 1:24-25

The sixth and final day has arrived of this most marvellous and massive programme of reconstruction, re-alignment, reconstitution and refurbishment in the history of this planet.

God has set Himself a target of six days for reasons which we hope to explain in the last chapter. He began with the planet totally dead, in complete darkness and all covered in water. Now after just five days He has established the environment which we now enjoy having introduced some new and temporary features such as a sun and a moon, day and night and some other items which were not there before the disaster.

The Earth we should remind ourselves is one ocean and one continent and God has already stocked the ocean with every type of creature and has also filled the skies with flying birds or fowls of the air as they are called. He does not mention at which point He introduced birds that do not fly such as chickens and ostriches. Maybe they are included in the creatures of the land?

Now He must turn His attention to the land mass which He has already named Earth. Already on the third day he has caused grass to grow all over the place and has introduced a wide variety of plants and trees but still there is nothing alive and moving on the land. This is to be His work in the first part of the sixth day. Because of its great importance to us as humans we are looking at the introduction of man in the image of God in a separate chapter.

As we have already noticed, God chooses His words very carefully in order to say exactly what He wishes to say. In reading the Bible with a desire to understand its meaning it is good advice to first offer up a little prayer asking the Holy Spirit, who told Moses what to write, to explain to our minds what He meant. This applies to the whole of the Bible, both the Old and New Testaments.

Understanding the verbal text mentally may not be enough to grasp the spiritual meaning of the words.

These two verses in Genesis 1:24-25 are so familiar that we do not always stop to ask God what they mean. One hopes in this little book to throw some light on what God was really saying. After all, it is what God says that matters, not what we mortal men say.

First of all we see that, "God says Let the Earth bring forth every living creature". He had said on day five, "Let the waters bring forth", which waters he himself named the sea. Now we do know that in the first chapter God tells us what He did and in the second chapter he tells some of the secrets of how He did it. He says there quite clearly that He made all birds that fly, all animals and of course man of the *dust of the earth*. All these creatures came from the soil. He does not however tell us how He made the sea creatures. Perhaps He keeps that as his little secret? Sufficient to say that it was He who made them. And so on this sixth day we are reminded again that God used the materials that were there, namely the soil, in order to make all animals. I cannot help but recall that it is the practice of God to use the materials then present, rather than manufacture something out of thin air. If there is something there God will use it. This is of great encouragement to Christians in the service for God. We remember that Jesus wanted to feed five thousand men, their womenfolk, and their children. He could have done it with nothing at all, or He could have made the stones of the ground into loaves. Instead, He chose to use one little lad's lunch. Never think that our puny gifts are too small for God to use to the glory of his name!

Next, I want to point out that frequent use of the word 'every'. Every living creature, every beast, every creeping thing and cattle. This should not be dismissed as a sweeping generalisation. God never makes such statements.   John says that: "All things were made by Him; without Him was nothing made that was made." (John 1:3)

This is repeated in Colossians 1 where the words 'all things' occur about seven times in relation to Creation.   Writing about the one they nailed to the cross Paul says:

> For by Him were all things created that are in heaven and that are in earth, visible and invisible...All things were created by Him and for Him:
> And He is before all things and by Him all things are held together.

Colossians 1:16-17

In God's language all things mean exactly that just as when He says *all* have sinned He makes no exceptions.

So then when God says that *every* living creature was made by Him out of the dust of the Earth his statement must not be lightly brushed aside.   God means precisely what He says.   Every form of life on Earth now is here in this temporary period because God made it and put it there.   In other words, no life evolved out of what was there previously.   But there is a strong connection as we shall see.

The next thing that we observe is that after stating that He created every living thing that creeps on the face of the Earth God selects three types of earth creatures for special mention.   They are the beast of the field, cattle and the creeping thing.   He then states that He made them naming the same three categories of created being but in a different order.   This is a common ploy in the Word of God.   First He lists in the order of importance, and then repeats them in the actual order in which He made them.   As a matter of interest to those who care to look it up, the same pattern is followed in the tabernacle in the wilderness.   First, the order of priorities to God, then the order of making the various items and finally, the order in which they were to be assembled.

To avoid repetition on our part we are only looking at the order in which God made the animals.

1.   The Beasts of the Field

These are called 'beasts of the Earth' in this second verse but the meaning is the same.   They are creatures belonging to the Earth or soil as opposed to creatures whose natural habitat is the sea or the sky. God made all such creatures from earwigs to elephants but is particularly thinking of four legged beasts who live in or on the land. There are creatures whose natural environment is the sea and who having gills draw their oxygen from the sea. These would not survive long on the land. Some creatures however live in the sea but have lungs and draw their supply of oxygen from the air. These can only survive if they can come up for air frequently.

The creatures we are now considering breathe air but belong to the soil. Many of them burrow into the Earth to make their homes underground. Badgers, rabbits, foxes and such like. Some live in holes on the river bank such as otters and beavers. They can swim and are at home in the water but they are creatures who belong to the land. Some of them need food produced by the soil. When they were first created they were given herbs to eat just like man.

There were no carnivores. Some of them could eat small insects and earthworms. God provided them by the million in order to keep the balance in nature.

But there are some notable absentees. There were now no dinosaurs. Gone are the fearsome Tyrannosaurus Rex, and no Triceratops charging about like tanks nor Pterodactyls swooping from the sky on their unsuspecting victim. It was the emergence of these beasts with their hostile attitudes under evil influence that brought about the disaster. Now God has left these huge monsters out altogether. In their place are much smaller creatures. There is no room on the planet for two hundred foot long monstrosities who kill just for the pleasure of doing harm, as well as for food. Instead there are lizards that stay quite small and are no threat to anyone. Triceratops are replaced by rhinos with only one horn. They will only attack when attacked or otherwise enraged. Huge birds of prey are left out completely. Today such animals as elephants, rhinos, hippos, giraffes, kangaroos are what God has introduced for His own pleasure. God loves to see a pride of lions roaming free. The sight of hippos rolling in the mud in the African sunshine gives God a great deal of pleasure I am sure. All creatures we are told are created for His pleasure. Even lions and bears were originally herbivores. They will all return to this state when Jesus comes back to reign if we read Isaiah 11.

2.   *Beasts of the Farm*

The second class singled out for special mention is 'cattle'. To us today the term cattle refers exclusively to the dairy herd. However, in those early days of the Bible cattle covers a much wider range of what we know as farm animals. The fact that God refers to them as 'cattle', 'after their kind' suggests that there were several species created on that day. The animals of the pre-historic ages were not made for man, because man in the image of God was not there. Now, however, the time has come for mankind to appear and everything has to be made ready for him.

Man will need transport, therefore God provides him with a horse. Easy to maintain and a pleasure to look after the horse will carry humans from point A to point B and some burdens as well. He will need a smaller beast just to carry burdens so God creates the donkey. A very loveable if at times stubborn animal. Horses and donkeys will need to drink water regularly and the journey may be long and no water to hand. God therefore invented the camel and dromedary. This beast can store water in one or even two humps and is ideal for long treks across desert wastes.

The man will also need a very strong beast to pull his plough or cart to carry bigger loads. God has thought about that and supplied the oxen. He will also not be expected to live only on water and will want a regular supply of milk. Hence God provides the remarkable cow. A brown cow eating green grass will give a daily supply of good nourishing white milk. Man tried a few years ago to feed grass cuttings into a machine and mix it with a substance something like the secretions from a cow's stomach. It took a factory the size of one of the sheds at Rover car works. The result was a powdered milk so expensive to produce and so inferior in quality that it could not be marketed and the project was abandoned. But of course a cow yielding milk needs a human hand to actually get the milk out of the cow and into the bucket. The cow is definitely for the benefit of mankind!

The man will also ultimately need clothing although not at the first. God comes up with a lovely creature that will grow the wool every year. It can be sheared and while the wool is made into yarn, the sheep will obligingly grow another coat. Goats supply a coarse hair which can be spun into fibre also to make clothes, while the skin of the goat when deceased makes an excellent bottle to hold wine or whatever the man wishes to store. The goat will also supply milk although not quite so profusely as the cow.

Now God specifically forbade the slaughter of animals for food until after the flood of Noah. He has provided man with freshwater fish, vegetables and an abundance of fruit and herbs to eat. The man cannot kill animals for food but God provides poultry which will lay eggs for food and can be eaten for meat.

Consider that there was only one continent and that man started in roughly what is now Iraq or Syria. The nearest contact with the ocean would be several thousand miles away and therefore fish would breed in the sea for many years before man even found out that the ocean was there let alone that there were fish in it and he could make boats from which to catch them. Fish then would be known to man as being in the rivers only and he would soon learn how to catch them to eat.

God has tried to think of everything that man will need. Transport, heavy workers' clothing. Flax and cotton will be grown and can be made into thread as well as the wool and goat hair fibre. And he has given man an abundance of good and varied food to eat. Such is the heart of a loving and caring God.

It is worth noticing that the only animals God would accept for sacrifice were from the flocks and herds. Bullocks, sheep and goats. Nothing could be offered to God either in worship or as a sin offering. The only full grown animal to be offered was a ram for consecration of the priest. God thus wished man to give back to him a little of what God had provided especially for the man's benefit and service. These cattle as we have said were not there previously because they were not needed. God introduces them with mankind in view.

3.   *Beasts of the Forest*

The third and final category named by God are called creeping things. I always wondered why God chose to mention creeping things because I assumed that they must be 'creepy crawlies'. I want to suggest that God had something else in mind. All these animals appear to be full grown. What exactly is a creeping thing?

The majority of beasts are four footed and go loping along the ground with no other use for their front paws except as an extra pair of legs to carry as much weight as the hind legs. Man on the other hand will walk on two legs and the other limbs are arms and hands to work with and not for walking. But notice the action of a monkey when walking. His front limbs are dangling on the ground and often touching the ground but he puts no weight on them. He can however use them for climbing trees and for holding things. Moving along the ground his action is halfway between loping and walking upright. You all know where this line of thought is leading I am sure. There is a creature midway between the elephant and the man. It is called a primate.

Now we do know evolution reached this stage just before the disaster. Here then is the astonishing truth. It took the evolutionary process probably two hundred million years to progress from crustaceans to primates. God now repeats the whole process in two days. Now however there is no time for anything to evolve. Each species, each stage has to be reproduced as a deliberate act of creation. But God keeps to the same sequence.

It has to be noticed that when speaking of creating sea creatures, the only species mentioned by name are the whales which are mammals not fish. The first major stage in evolution was when creatures who lived in the sea began to emerge as having lungs to draw their oxygen from the air above the ocean. The final stage of evolution was the emergence of primates.

From creatures whose life began in the sea right up to creatures who were very nearly man, God has repeated the whole wonderful development in two days with a series of creative acts which re-established the order of Creation and brought the whole story right up to the point where man could be introduced to the environment specifically created for him.

Let us not rob God of the credit for this great work, of Creation. Only God could have done it at all, let alone in the time which He allotted to Himself. This is the glory of God the Creator. And He definitely did it all in six days.

Chapter Eleven
Day Six (Part 2) – The Image of God

And God said, Let us make man in our image after our likeness; and let them have dominion over the fish of the sea and over the fowl of the air, and over the cattle, and over all the earth, and over every creeping thing that creeps upon the earth.
So God created man in his own image; in the image of God created he him; male and female created he them.

Genesis 1:26-27

The climax of this great six day terrestrial extravaganza is now about to be reached. No inventor ever revealed his latest brainchild to a waiting world with more pleasure than God as He now prepares to make His greatest creation of all time. He was going to make the unthinkable, namely a creature capable of thinking and behaving like God himself. We have to consider how God did it, and why He did it, and why He expected the experiment to fail initially but had made plans how to deal with its failure. I would like to break these two verses into three parts.

1.   *A Divine Announcement*
"And God said, Let us make man in our image". Here is consultation at the highest level with Father, Son and Holy Spirit as we now call them, debating together and deciding that the time has now come to introduce their latest and greatest creation. Let us make man, suggests a conferring together for all the Trinity is involved in this exercise. It is the first indication in Genesis that God is more than just one person.

But what exactly does it mean to make anything in the image of God? You may recall that earlier in our studies we reported that the invisible God assumed visible form and that this person is described as the image of God. The Eternal Son, as He became known, was not made *in* the image of God, he *was* the image of God. He was not merely like God, he *was* God. There the image is an *eikon* and shows that the Son is the exact reproduction of the character and personality of the Invisible God. They were two persons yet they were one and the same. The Son would always do everything exactly the way God required because he thought along the same lines and would without fail always arrive at the same conclusion. Now with the co-operation of the Holy Spirit they wish to produce a being who will also want to do things God's way as being always the best way. If a man thinks like God, he will have the values and priorities of God and will desire to please and obey God at all times.

The word for image now used is quite different from the *eikon* used for the Son of God. The Hebrew word used means a shadow or resemblance of God. It suggests a reflection in a mirror which at times may be only a feeble reflection. A creature modelled loosely upon God. Let me explain.

God is as we have seen a tripartite being. We call them Father, Son and Spirit. That is because that is how they are described in the New Testament. The man created will also therefore be a three part being. His three parts will be body, soul and spirit. To put it in simple every day language man will operate on three levels, the physical, the emotional and the spiritual. He gets these three levels from God Himself.

The invisible Spirit which we call God is comparable to the soul of God. The soul is the seat of feelings, emotions, and inner thoughts and desires. The soul is never seen but is the real person inside us thinking and planning. It can be pleased and it can be hurt without anyone else knowing how it feels. God plans and has wishes or will as we call it. He is very pleased with some things and very hurt at other times without showing His real feelings. One way in which he is easily hurt is when someone takes a tree, which God himself provided and cuts it down. The man then proceeds to take part of that tree and cut and shape it to look like an animal or even a man. He paints and decorates it and then announces that this thing which he has made is God who blesses all His crops and family. Now it remains an inanimate object incapable of seeing, hearing, thinking, speaking or doing anything. Whether it is made of wood or stone it is dead. God says in Isaiah that He is a jealous God and very much hurt when someone refuses to give God the credit for His Creation and says that a dumb idol did it. He is even more hurt when someone says that nobody did the creation because it just did it itself. This is the soul of the invisible God who is never deflected from His purpose.

When the men came to translate the New Testament from its original Greek into English they came across the word *theios*. This was a slight variation from the normal word for God which was *theos*. If they translated *theios* as deity which would have been right they would create the impression that God was to be lumped together with all the Roman, Greek, Egyptian and Babylonian deities which were merely idols. To avoid confusing God with idols they invented the word 'Godhead'.

Godhead therefore conveys the identity of the one true God, the only true and living God, creator and sustainer of the universe and giver of life. We are called upon to give Him credit for the great work which He has done. If as we suggest life evolved on the Earth over millions of years it was still God who made the Earth and put the original forms of life on the planet in whatever forms that life came. God is the Creator and he is one person in three aspects while at the same time He is three persons in one.

If the Godhead is in three aspects then the Father is the soul of the Godhead. He is the source of all its thoughts and purposes, the secret of His will and desires, and the seat of all His intentions.

If the Father is the soul of the Godhead then the Son is the body of the Godhead. We say this very reverentially. The Son is the visible God, the physical and discernible revelation of the Godhead. If the Father is the origin of all the thoughts then the Son is the purveyor of all the actions. The Son is the one declared to be the creator of all things. A body performs all the actions which the mind dictates. There is trouble in the body only if there is a breakdown of communication between the two parts. And between Father and Son there has never been any lack of co-ordination. Let me elaborate a little.

God is said to have the following manners of a body.

His *eyes* are upon the righteous.
His *ears* are open to their cry.
The *face* of the Lord is against them that do evil.
All these features are quoted in Psalm 34.
The *mouth* of the Lord speaks great things
The *arms* of the everlasting God are there for support

The *arm* of the Lord is there for salvation
The *hands* of the Lord are there to uphold and to guide
The *feet* of the Lord will tread down his enemies.

Eyes, ears, face, mouth, arms, hands and feet. All these members are attributed to God yet He probably has none of them if we could see Him. They are symbolic representations of His characteristics. They belong to the visible God, the Son of God who sees, hears, speaks, upholds and guides. All the actions taken by God are done by the Son who is the tangible God. He is given credit for creating all things simply because He performs all the actions at the suggestion of His Father. We speak as human beings trying to understand the nature of the Godhead. But we must remember that man is modelled upon God and not the other way round.

There is also of course the Spirit of God. There is a very subtle difference between God the Spirit and the Spirit of God. For God himself is a Spirit as we have seen at the beginning. His own spirit however is the breath of God, the emanation of His own life and nature. We do not see the Spirit but we do see the evidence of His workings. The Spirit is involved in the realms of the spiritual and this means that He is in charge of such things as faith, hope, love and prayer and worship.

This then is the original Godhead and still functioning as the Eternal God. A mind, a body and a spirit working together as one great unity. This is the model God was going to use in order to make man. His supreme act of Creation.

2. *The Divine Action*

So he made man in his own image. Male and female created he them.

We have already observed that God made man with three aspects to operate on three levels. In the mind of God man would be spirit, soul and body. To the mind of man it is the other way round. Man is said to be a body, a soul and a spirit. Physical things come first, emotional things next and spiritual things come last. That is not the way God intended. Let us compare man with the other things God had created already before man.

Angels are spirits, as we have noted. They worship God and they serve God as directed. But they are not souls in the sense that they are not independent minds. An angel cannot choose whether or how to obey God. They are created to carry out the orders of God without question. If an angel disobeys God there is no way back for him to obtain forgiveness or to repent. He, therefore, has no soul to save as we understand it. Redemption is not on offer. He is a spiritual being but not a soul with a mind of his own. The angel will have a body but it is not of importance since he is not tied to it like man. An angel seems able to assume a bodily shape according to whatever task is appointed to him. Thus, if an angel came down to Earth to deliver a message he could assume the body of a man. But he is able to move instantly from one part of the Heavens to another by the fastest speed of all, the speed of thought. Heaven does not know the physical limitations which we endure on Earth. An angel therefore is not a spirit, soul and body. He is a spirit, not a soul and with a body of no great importance.

Animals on the other hand are very different from angels. Animals, which include all created beings from fishes upwards to primates, have bodies. They can eat, sleep, walk and produce offspring. Angels cannot have any children. Although we speak of an angel as 'he', an angel is in fact neither he nor she but sexless. Animals on the other hand are largely physical beings and have all the characteristics of a physical existence. It is noticeable that the higher up one gets on the animal scale the greater the tendency for animals to stick together as families. This will show itself fully in man for whom God intended the family unit to be the corner stone of society.

Animals have a sort of soul, in that they do have minds of their own and feelings although not subject to the full range of human emotions. They do not, for instance, have a guilt complex. All the same, the phrase 'living creature' means a living soul and is used for animals just as for humans.

The biggest difference between animals and humans however is that animals do not have a spiritual nature. No fish, bird or animal is able to go to church and worship God. They cannot offer praise or thanksgiving to the Almighty who created them, nor can they sing hymns. An animal is not able to engage in prayer either in request or in supplication. There is just no form of spiritual communication between the Creator and the creatures which He has brought into existence. While they obey their Creator and trust Him to meet their needs, this is not by conscious choice.

We turn then to the making of man as the supreme act of Creation. First, God Himself has a body and through that body He can make and create anything He wishes. He, therefore, gives to the man a body. The body is the means by which we communicate with the world around us. Through the five senses we see things, hear things, touch, taste and smell things and so are made aware of what is happening. By means of its various members we express ourselves. Thus man has a voice which can speak, converse, teach others, sing and so on. We have arms and hands by which we can do many things. We can play a musical instrument, dig the garden, build a house, make objects out of materials available, paint pictures and so on. What we want to do we can do with our hands. Our arms enable us to hold our babies and many other things. With our legs we can walk, run, swim play football and express ourselves in many ways. The members of our physical bodies enable us to make anything we wish and do as we choose.

This corresponds with the activities of the Son who is the visible body of the Godhead. The main difference is that we are limited by our lack of knowledge and resources. The Son of God has no such limitation. We have to study to acquire knowledge. He already has it.

But a body must have a mind to control it and God has given us a mind which is part of the soul. Man has not got a soul he *is* a living soul. That soul though unseen is the seat and source of all our thoughts and desires.

The mind which God has given us is as superior to the mind of an animal as is his body. Our mind is capable like God of sitting down and working things out thinking things through. It would be pointless giving man a mouth by which he can express his thoughts if he had no thoughts to express. Man can take pieces of paper and calculate how many bricks he will need, and how much sand, cement and timber and then go out and build anything he wishes from a dog kennel to a skyscraper block. He is given the ability. He can construct a rocket to go outside our solar system and cameras to put on it. Aeroplanes are not a problem any longer, only an expense. Bridges and boats, trains and cars are all being constructed all the time. God has given man the mental capacity to work all these things out and to make them.

The mind of man can also take a problem and weigh up the arguments for and against and arrive at a solution or judgement. God has given him the facility to make his own decisions. In other words God has given man freedom of choice. He has given him free will which is not given to any other creature in the universe. Angels have no free will but must do as they are told. Animals do not have the freedom to choose as man has.

Given that man has the capacity to make decisions God expects him to make them. This opens up the enormous subject of the will of God which we are not going to explore now. Suffice it to say that if we want to sin God will let us. It is our choice. But He will warn us of the consequences. If we believe the Word of God that there is an offer of eternal life for us, then we shall receive it. If we do not want it then He will never force it upon us.

The mind is the engine room of the soul, the power house by which the hidden person within us translates its innermost thoughts, plans and intentions into action, reaction or even inaction.

Jesus once said that as a man thinks in his heart so is he. This is the soul of a man revealing its true nature. If the human being is far superior to animals in bodily activities he is even more so when it comes to translating his motives and intentions into actions. A human being covers the entire gamut of emotions from heights of happiness to depths of despair. Certain animals show traces of these emotions as when a dog wags its tail because it is pleased. However I have never known a dog go out and deliberately throw itself under a bus, or a cat rush out and drown itself because it felt that life was no longer worth living. Deep depression is one of the emotions which are foreign to animals. The reason is because of the fundamental difference between the two as souls.

The third thing that God gave to man was the 'breath of life'. Now I must confess I do not know how He imparted life to other creatures. Whether it was by breathing on them or touching them or just speaking to them. I do know that for man and only for man we read that God made man a full size body and knelt down and breathed into his nostrils the breath of life and the man became a living soul. The very first kiss of life. When God brings back thousands of millions of people from the dead He will only need to speak the word and they will appear with a resurrected body. Creating resurrected beings will be no more difficult for him than creating the many creatures that had existed before the demise of the dinosaurs.

When God breathed the breath of life into Adam He imparted to him part of His own nature, namely the spirit of life. God and man could converse together and enjoy sweet communion because there was no barrier of sin between them. Man could offer worship to the living God and God could accept it. He could talk to God, which was the original form of prayer because God was there in the cool of every day and he could understand all that God said to him.

Man had received the nature of God which included a desire to be clean in body and a love of fresh food. In the First Letter of Paul to Timothy we read that cleanliness is next to godliness. This means that cleanliness in body and clothing is the first outward sign of a change of heart towards God very often.

Having the nature of God meant also that he had the love of God within him for all the creatures that God had created. Adam could love his wife when she was made and also his children when they came along. The nature of God is essentially love for all.

The nature of God also included a conscience. Adam would know, as all men must know deep down inside, when something is wrong and not in accordance with the mind of God. Whether he had a full awareness of what was holy we do not know but he was certainly aware of what was not holy. And so even people who have never read the Bible are aware that some things are definitely wrong and should not be done.

Thus God had made a being with many aspects of the divine nature. He would operate on three levels: spiritual, emotional and physical. If the top level was right, and the man was in tune with God then the mind or soul would be right and would control the actions of the body. This was the clear intention of the Creator. He had made a being modelled upon himself who could indeed think and act like himself in every way.

We must stress, however, that this is the man as originally created. A perfect Creation in a perfect world without sin. Things would change dramatically the moment the man disobeyed the Maker.

3. The Divine Appointment
Before concluding this chapter on the making of man we have to consider why God made him at all.

And God said, Let them have dominion over the fish of
the sea, and over the fowl of the air, and over the cattle
and over all the earth, and over every creeping thing
that creepeth on the earth.

Genesis 1:26

It is a very comprehensive statement of the authority given to both Adam and Eve, for they were both created in the image of God and given joint dominion over all the other things that God had created. God put them in charge and looked to them to run the planet his way. The extent of this appointment is to be considered now.

In the sequence of events detailed in Genesis 1:4-26, God, first of all, says what He is going to do, then why He is going to do it and then just gets on and does it. We are therefore considering the *why* a little out of its order. Why did God want to make a creature like man?

Contrary to much public belief, God is neither careless nor callous concerning His creatures. He regards the planet as one great zoological garden, one vast safari park, and has a high regard for the welfare of every created thing in it. When He created a breeding pair of otters He had a reason and was going to follow the future progress of all otters thereafter and seek their best interests. When He made a cob and a pen He was going to safeguard the interests of all future generations of swans. That is God's way. He himself saw to it that initially as created there was nothing that His creatures could eat that would harm them. There were no poisonous fungi or berries and no death dealing insects. No animal or bird was going to seek them out and kill them for food because all were originally made vegetarians.

The whole scenario of nature was designed for peace and prosperity. God never makes anything and then just leaves it to its own devices. He has a natural concern for all His creatures. You have only to read the closing six chapters or so of Job to see His view that all the world is His family as created by Him. He tells of a family of wild goats that are expecting a happy event and must look after them. He speaks of a pride of lions that are hungry and He must send them some food. All created things are His responsibility. That is God in his providential role as provider. All creatures great and small were meant to live in peace and harmony with each other including mankind. It was the coming in of evil that brought about the law of the jungle.

It was essential therefore that if He made man in the image of God, he would be appointed curator of this great zoo. To fulfil his role as gardener and zoo keeper, man must run things along the same lines as God Himself. That means that he too must have a natural care for living things and not wish to see any of them come to any harm. God is love by nature and that love should be shown to all God's created beings. Such love would be pleasing to God.

At the same time God is light and that includes the light of truth and holiness. The man should therefore have a love for honesty, truth, integrity. In short, he must love righteousness. Before a man can love God's creatures he must love God Himself.

Love is a matter of personal choice. God loved man and all that He had created. He loved the world which He had made. But the man must choose for himself whether he is going to reciprocate that love or whether to accept it and not bother to return it. God wants love to beget love. He could quite easily give the man and woman the ability to love but he would not force them to use it. That must be their choice.

God in the beginning made them male and female. God wanted them as a matter of choice to love all of His created things including their fellow men and women.

The two dominant sides of God's love are seen in Adam and Eve. The male side is the love of a Father. Strong love begetting children and protecting them and providing for them. That is the male side of love. The word husband originally was "houseband" meaning the band that held the household together. The man went out to work and built up his family with providential love. The female love is the love of a mother. This is not weak, but is tender and caring and very practical. Both male and female love represent the two sides of the love of God for all his created beings. Love is to look after someone's best interests. God has the best interests of all at heart. He wanted the man and woman together to look after his great handiwork.

Thus the sixth day ended with God giving the man and his wife dominion and authority over all fishes, birds and animals which he had brought into being as creator in six days.

Chapter Twelve

Day Seven – Time to Take a Rest

Thus the heavens and the earth were finished and all the host of them.
And on the seventh day God ended his work which he had made; and
he rested on the seventh day from all his work which he had made.
And God blessed the seventh day and sanctified it: because in it he had
rested from all his work which God had created and made.

Genesis 2:1-3

Never did the Sun rise on such a glorious and tranquil scene as on this the first full day of the new Creation! In just six days God had transformed the Earth from total chaos to a thriving cosmos, teeming with life. Whether each day was literally twenty-four hours as we now know it or a little longer is neither here nor there. The fact is that each day was one period of daylight and one period of darkness and God did it in six days. No one else could have done it if only because no one else was capable and because no one else was there apart from angels. I have never heard any one suggest that the angels did it and man was not created until the sixth day. It is unreasonable to even think that it did it all by itself within the time allowed. Therefore, we must give all glory to God the Almighty the Creator. He says here in the first verse of the second chapter that thus the Heavens and the Earth were finished and all the host of them. God had seemingly made his last solar system. He had accomplished more than just the reclamation of the Earth. He had completed his work in the Creation of the universe. The re-creation was done in six days but God created something else very special on the seventh day. He created a rest.

We must observe that God says three things about this seventh day. First, He rested on it, then He blessed it and finally, He sanctified or hallowed it.

Rest in the Scripture does not mean idleness. God is never idle. It means that He had made what He set out to make and now He is going to sit back and let it work for him. Let us give an illustration of what He means. An engineer makes a lathe which will turn and shape a piece of wood. He is not going then to put it into a showroom and continue to make chair legs with his hands. He made it to use and now he is going to let the machine do the work. Similarly a farmer acquires a combine harvester. He is not going to store it away in a barn and continue to use a horse drawn plough or a sickle to cut the corn. He is going to use it and in that sense he is resting while working because the machine is doing the work. This is the principle adopted by God. The Earth is full of living and growing things. Let them now continue to thrive and progress. All God needs to do is to watch their progress and prosperity. It reminds me of a landscape gardener. When he has finished the layout of the garden he just has to watch over the trees and shrubs and give them space. They will then grow themselves.

There is a more serious teaching to the rest if we were to follow it through the Bible. Two and half thousand years later God had built up a nation of Israel to be His people. He offers them his own rest. The rest is built into the Mosaic law by the fourth commandment. Remember the Sabbath day to keep it holy or clean. This was a command with punishment of death by stoning for the Sabbath breaker. A bit harsh you might think because it made breaking of the Sabbath equal to murder and adultery in terms of punishment.

But God had ordered them to take a rest on the seventh day. Work for six days and then take a rest. The theory behind the teaching is that the Earth will run for six thousand years approximately and then the seven thousandth year will be for the Earth a Sabbath of rest, a millennium during which Messiah will reign in peace and the Earth will enjoy unparalleled prosperity. The thousand year millennium is perfectly true although you have to wait until Revelations 20 before you learn that the rest will be a thousand years. If the theory is true, then the Earth had two thousand years until the call of Abraham and a further two thousand years until the death of Jesus Christ. In which case we are getting very near to the end of the third two thousand year spell. Now that is the theory regarding the six days of the Earth and a seventh day of rest. I personally accept the theory to be true although the Bible does not actually say so. It is my firm belief that God always intended the Earth to have a Sabbath of rest for a thousand years and that the time is drawing very near for it to begin.

Israel, as we know failed, and while we do not wish to go into the matter too deeply here, a further offer was made to the Church of an enjoyment of rest by the new people of God and this is outlined in Hebrews 4. The rest for the Church made up of both Jews and Gentiles is not for a thousand years but for all eternity.

The Church is administered under grace and not under the rule of Law. Therefore, there is a major change when it comes to keeping the Sabbath. Instead of working for six days and giving God the seventh, God asks the New Testament Church to give him the first day and he will bless the remainder of the week. "The morrow after the Sabbath" is a common phrase in Moses. It is the day when the sheaf of the first fruits was to be waved and speaks of Resurrection. In celebration of the death and Resurrection of Jesus Christ, God asks Christians to give to Him the first day of the week.

Secondly, God blessed the seventh day. On days five and six He blessed all the creatures he had made. 'Be fruitful and multiply' He said to fishes, birds, animals and to Adam and Eve. Now for the first time He blesses the day. I believe that the nation that is prepared to give God the Sabbath as one that can be used for Him and His worship and service will be blessed of God.

Thirdly, He sanctified the seventh day. God hallowed it to be a holy day. It is the only item of Creation to be declared holy. All other things God said when He made them that they were good. He sums it all up by saying that He saw all things that He had created and made and behold it was *very good*. Creation was very good in that there was no trace of evil in it. Good is always opposed to evil in the Bible. There was nothing offensive to God and nothing harmful to his creatures. Now however he declares the seventh day to be not merely good but holy. What is the difference between good and holy? Well, something good is anything that does good to the receivers. There was an abundance of fresh food, fresh air and fresh water. Even the daylight was good and beneficial to all. But holiness is when God sees it set apart. In the sight of God a thing is holy if it is set aside for him like the holy furniture of the Tabernacle. God says that He has given us richly all things to enjoy but the Ark and the Altar He says are holy to Him. They are mine and must not be defiled. So as far as the

Sabbath is concerned keep it clean and set apart for God. This is required of all God's people. It covers all creation.

Our story is nearly finished. The Earth is transformed from darkness to light, from death to life and is now up and running. The ensuing tale is one of man's failure and of God's faithfulness. As the number of fishes, birds and animals continued to rise so would the number of men and women with the intention that they would continue to have rule over all created things. If man was to run the planet in a manner pleasing to God then he should be able to pass one simple test.

And so God gave him a *promise*. 'Of every tree in the garden you may freely eat'. He did not have to ask God's permission or even to tell him. He could enjoy all that God had provided. This is an important principle of God's dealings with mankind. He gives us richly all things to enjoy and he gives them free of charge. This included the Tree of Life but Adam never asked God what would happen if he ate of that tree.

There was also a *prohibition*. 'But of the Tree of Knowledge of Good and Evil you may not eat'. This was not a knowledge of science or of sex but of spiritual things such as what constituted good and what was evil. God was keeping that choice to Himself. At that time, Adam was not aware that such a thing as evil existed elsewhere in the universe. God wanted to keep it that way.

Also it has to be said that in every game there must be some rules or neither the players nor the spectators will know what is allowed and what is not. Why then is it thought so difficult when God introduced some basic rules in the game of life? Therefore, there must be some things which God says we must not do. Having to decide what was good and what was evil was one choice which God did not want Adam to have to make.

There was also a *penalty*. The day you eat thereof you will surely die. Now what did God mean by that? The tree was not poisonous and therefore it was not the eating that would kill him. Was it punishment? To strike him dead for eating a fruit which by the way was not an apple would be very harsh indeed methinks.

No it was not punishment for a crime. So what was God saying?

God was stating the most basic of all principles in the Bible: it was not the fruit that would kill him nor the eating of it, but the act of putting out his hand to take it knowing that God had said he must not do it. That would constitute an act of disobedience and therefore a sin and sin always separates from God. That is what God was telling him. He would die instantly, not physically because he was going to live to be nine hundred and thirty years old, but he would die spiritually because his communication with God would be severed. Only the shedding of blood of a substitute would restore that communion. Abel worked it out but Adam did not. Spiritually, he died the moment he sinned. This is what God was trying to tell him. Adam would become a body and soul but his spiritual nature was dead. In time he would die physically and if he died without that sin being forgiven and removed then eventually he would die eternally.

Well, as we know he did sin and was denied access to the Tree of Life by being turned out of the Garden. By one man, sin entered into the world and death by sin as God knew it would. In time God would put into operation the great plan of redemption and send His own Son as a man to obey God to the limit and allow Himself to be a human sacrifice perfect in every way and acceptable to God. This sacrifice would provide the basis for worship and would provide the blood of atonement. It will need another book bigger than this one to explain all this but the reader can always go to the Gospel of John, the Letter to the Romans 5, and the Letter to Hebrews.

We have written in detail about what God is like, how evil entered God's perfect world through the fallen Angel, and led to the disaster which overtook the dinosaurs. We have seen what God says about how He recreated the world and put on it man in his own image. But the reader who seeks further knowledge of the truth about this or any other matter must go himself or herself to the Bible and read it for themselves. May the Spirit of God guide the thoughts of all who thus genuinely seek the Truth as it is in Christ Jesus.

> *Howbeit when he, the Spirit of truth, is come, he will guide you into all truth.*
>
> John 16:13

Epilogue

Heaven and earth shall pass away, but my words shall not pass way.
                                                              Matthew 24:35

These words of Jesus are among the most astonishing words spoken by a man who was always astonishing people. In a passage foretelling future events on Earth Jesus claims divine authority in saying that even when the Earth as we know it has ceased to exist His words will remain.

In writing this little book we have adopted one principle. The star speaker in the debate on Creation is the Creator Himself. We have tried to quote exactly what God has said in His Word and to try in some feeble way to explain what we think He means. There is no intention on our part to substitute our own views for the statements made by God. It would be the height of folly to imagine that we could ever express anything more truthfully or more forcefully than the Almighty. In trying to explain things we have probably left many things still unexplained. While trying to answer some questions we have doubtless posed more questions that need answers.

Some Bible lovers will undoubtedly hold differing views. To such we would say that the Word of God is the only solid based truth, and all that men say or write by way of explanation or opinion will only ever represent the personal understanding of the individual. We all have finite and limited minds and are together seeking to arrive at a better understanding of the Truth. If we have made someone think again about the story of Creation in Genesis, then please go back to the Bible and read it again prayerfully. Perhaps the Spirit of God who wrote it will guide your thoughts into a better grasp than our own, which we do not pretend to be perfect. When we reach the heavenly shores and begin our eternal existence I am sure we will all understand more perfectly truths and passages which have baffled us down here.

It is with the prayer that these imperfect thoughts of ours will lead some more deeply into a better understanding of the Word of God that this book is sent out.

May the Lord richly bless all who read.